DO YOU THINK I'M BEAUTIFUL?

ANSWERING THE QUESTION
Every WOMAN ASKS

ANGELA THOMAS

Leader Guide written by Judi Slayden Hayes

LifeWay Press®
Nashville, Tennessee

Published by LifeWay Press®
© 2007 • Angela Thomas
Second printing June 2009

Derived from the book *Do You Think I'm Beautiful?* © 2003 by Angela Thomas
and published with consent of Thomas Nelson Publishers.

ISBN 978-1-4158-6048-3
Item 005099267

This book is a resource in the subject area Personal Life of the Christian Growth Study Plan.
Course CG-1312

Dewey Decimal Classification: 248.843
Subject Heading: WOMEN \ CHRISTIAN LIFE

Unless otherwise noted, Scripture quotations are from the Holy Bible, New International Version,
copyright © 1973, 1978, 1984 by International Bible Society. Scripture quotations marked NKJV are from
the New King James Version. Copyright © 1979, 1980, 1982, Thomas Nelson, Inc., Publishers. Scripture
quotations marked The Message are from THE MESSAGE. Copyright © by Eugene H. Peterson, 1993,
1994, 1995. Used by permission of NavPress Publishing Group. Scripture quotations marked KJV are
from the King James Version of the Bible. Scripture quotations marked CEV are from the Contemporary
English Version. Copyright © 1991, 1992, 1995 by American Bible Society. Used by permission.

To order additional copies of this resource, write LifeWay Church Resources
Customer Service; One LifeWay Plaza; Nashville, TN 37234-0113;
fax order to (615) 251-5933; e-mail *orderentry@lifeway.com;*
call toll-free (800) 458-2772; order online at *www.lifeway.com;*
or visit the LifeWay Christian Store serving you.

Printed in the United States of America

Leadership and Adult Publishing
LifeWay Church Resources
One LifeWay Plaza
Nashville, Tennessee 37234-0175

CONTENTS

ABOUT THE AUTHOR

ANGELA THOMAS is a mother, best-selling author, speaker, and teacher. She is a woman in desperate pursuit of God. Her determination to know God on an intimate level and her dedication to studying the Bible have taught her many truths, some discovered through tears and some in times of joy.

Angela graduated from the University of North Carolina at Chapel Hill with a double major in economics and television production. She began full-time work in the field of transportation, but it was her avocation as part-time youth director that led her to enroll at Dallas Theological Seminary. She earned her Master's degree in Dallas and moved to North Carolina to become a minister to senior high girls. Marriage and babies followed not long after, providing Angela with much joy ... and much change.

Angela wrote her first book, *Prayers for Expectant Mothers*, during her fourth pregnancy and followed it with *Prayers for New Mothers*. Her 2001 Focus on the Family release, *Tender Mercy for a Mother's Soul*, became a best seller.

Angela's writing had grown naturally out of her day-to-day life as a mother and as a woman. "I promised God I would tell the truth about my life and His work within me. My writing is just an extension of that. I'm really a storyteller, sharing out of my own life experiences."

Angela's other best-selling writings include *Do You Think I'm Beautiful?*, *When Wallflowers Dance*, *Beautiful* (for young women), and *Wild About You* (for students). Her latest release is *My Single Mom Life*.

Today, Angela speaks at conferences, retreats, and Bible studies across the country. Audiences enthusiastically respond to her practical, relevant discussions, and she instantly bonds with all types of women. Without the wrappings of pretense or pride, Angela tells it like it is ... and how it can be.

Angela and her children, AnnaGrace, William, Grayson, and Taylor, reside in Knoxville, Tennessee. Angela, a single mom, is heavily involved at Two Rivers Church, where her family has attended since moving to Knoxville.

JUDI SLAYDEN HAYES wrote the Leader Guide for this study. Judi is a writer and an editor. She lives in Mt. Juliet, Tennessee, with husband, David, and their cat, Chapel. Judi and David are members of First Baptist Church, Nashville. Judi loves to travel and has visited 37 countries on 5 continents. Whether on the road or at home, she always has a pile of books to read.

INTRODUCTION

Welcome to a study of the Father's amazing love for each of us. God's love for you is personal. He is wildly in love with you, and His love never ends, no matter where life has taken you or what circumstances you have faced.

This unfathomable love of God brings out the best in every woman who gives herself to Him. The more we know our hearts and the compelling love of God, the more fully we live for His glory. We become more grateful, giving to those around us the passionate love so freely given to us. So much growth happens when we live in the power and security of that love. I want you to know fresh passion for God in these weeks.

I've wanted to dance for as long as I can remember. I took ballet in the first grade, but my teacher moved away. In college, I enrolled in beginning ballet, but we were all a little too late. Prima donna-ness had passed us by. Still I love to dance, and lack of training doesn't keep me down. I guess that's why the notion of dancing in the arms of God speaks to me. Dancing is for celebration, fun, and romance. I love the thought of sharing all that with the God of heaven.

Some people struggle with *dancing* and *God* in the same sentence. Here's my take on it. As soon as my babies could pull themselves up, they would bob and sway to the beat. Their great delight over anything made their feet move, their eyes twinkle, and their arms wave. It seems the Creator created dance as a celebration of delight. Remember David in the Bible? He was so overwhelmed by God's love that he danced. So I'm OK with illustrating our relationship to God through the pictures and thoughts of dancing in His arms. I hope it speaks to some of the longings deep inside you as well. If not, take it as a metaphor for how very much God loves you.

When I wrote *Do You Think I'm Beautiful?* I thought I was just writing my own longings. It turns out I had described the feminine soul. Almost every day we hear from a woman somewhere whose life, marriage, or heart has been changed by this message of God's rescuing, protecting, providing love. I pray this study based on the book will impact your heart with an embracing love that gives peace, hope, and purpose.

At times I will call you to introspection and self-description. Those things tend to make me squirm, and I never understood why until recently. When I'm asked to describe myself, I squirm because I haven't known who I am. I have been afraid to look and be disappointed. I hope you push past the discomfort and explore who you are. Write what God says and does so you can remember His answers and His leading.

I will also call you to more prayer than you may be accustomed. Real change happens in prayer. A weak woman becomes an overcomer in prayer. I want you to hear God more than I want you to hear anything else. Learn to know His voice.

I am praying for God to astound you with His presence, power, and grace. I hope you dance the dance of your life in the Father's arms.

With love,

Angela

Do You Think I'm Beautiful?

If there is a question attached

to the soul of a woman, maybe it's,

"Do you think I'm beautiful?"

What a journey we are getting ready to take! I am so excited to run alongside you for these next weeks. I have been praying like crazy for God to speak to your heart in amazing, God-sized ways.

This week we're going back to junior high and high school. Reliving a little of what many of us have tried to forget. Remembering can be delightful, but sometimes remembering can be painful. Ask God to give your memories clarity and purpose. Ask Him for the courage to be truthful. Sometimes the most powerful insights come because we have finally let the truth out of its hiding place.

Do you have some junior-high or high-school pictures of yourself lying around, or maybe some yearbooks stuffed into a box in the attic? This would be a great time to pull them out. It's amazing how the power of a picture can help you remember.

VIEWER GUIDE

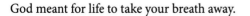

God meant for life to take your breath away.

Sometimes because of the _____ _____

Sometimes because of the _____ _____

When you are _____, you miss everything.

"Oh, God, do you think I'm beautiful?"

"Yes, you were beautiful to me when I dreamed you up."

"The king is enthralled by your beauty."
Psalm 45:11

The God of heaven calls you _____—and it's true.

DAY 1

YOUR STORY

For many of us, before we knew what hit us, we were had. Our minds and esteem had been shaped and manipulated by junior-high words and high-school heartbreak. We never saw it coming nor had any idea it would matter for a lifetime. What they thought of us or never thought of us did its work in our heads, and now we're trying to undo the damage and find the beautiful woman who got lost in the scuffle.

Here's a little bit of my story:

I've worn glasses since I was 18 months old. My first pair had cat-eye shaped frames, and everyone thought I looked so cute in them. "Oh, look at that little baby with glasses. Isn't she the sweetest thing?" Then I began to grow, and for about a year I had to wear a patch over my right eye to make the left one stronger. ... It didn't work. It caused my weaker eye to become the dominant one. ... Don't you know I was a stunner in the Captain Hook patch with cat-eye glasses?

Eventually, in elementary school, classmates and neighborhood kids tagged me "four eyes." One of maybe three "four eyes" in the entire school. Worse, I wore wire-rim, stop-sign-shaped glasses. How cool can a girl be with traffic signs in front of her eyes? Not very. And a few years later ... we added three and a half years of braces. *Railroad tracks. Tinsel teeth.* ... Thick bottle caps before my eyes, tin on my teeth, and—to make things as awful as possible—I was smart. In case you've forgotten, girls don't want to be smart in junior high—they want to be pretty.

By those tender junior high years, I knew for sure that beauty had eluded me. My best friend, Carla, was beautiful. Some senior guy even asked her to the prom when we were in the eighth grade. The eighth grade! ... Carla was at the high school prom, and I was probably at home writing a paper. Yep, there were many beautiful girls at my school, but I was not among them. I could do algebra and remember the answers for history tests. I actually did all of my homework and turned it in on time. The other day, Carla reminded me that I used to make up practice tests, take the tests, and then grade them—all to prepare for the actual thing. What a dweeb!

All I really wanted was to look like everyone else, but my circumstances wouldn't cooperate. Long, thick, straight hair that I styled with two barrettes every day of my young life. Braces that seemed destined to be a permanent part of my smile. The doom of four eyes forever. Don't get the wrong impression; no one ever called me ugly; no one ever laughed in my face. It's just that no one ever noticed.[1]

I'm sure you can understand how those years shaped my thoughts about beauty. I had always been the girl no one noticed. The afterthought when compliments were handed out. The girl no one wanted to "go steady" with. The brainy nerd who tried hard to please.

Your story may be nothing like mine. I have girlfriends who remember strong middle- and high-school years. They have amazing testimonies of family, spiritual growth, and fun memories. So whatever those years were for you, let's start there. It's your turn to relive those foundational years. What is your growing up story?

Describe your elementary years. _____
_____
_____
_____

Were you a leader or a follower? _____

What were your favorite childhood games? _____
_____
_____
_____

What did you do with your summer vacations? _____
_____
_____
_____

Describe a couple of your closest friends back then. _____
_____
_____
_____

For you created my inmost being;
    you knit me together in my mother's womb.
I praise you because I am fearfully and wonderfully made;
    your works are wonderful, I know that full well.
My frame was not hidden from you when I was made in the secret place.
When I was woven together in the depths of the earth, your eyes saw my unformed body.
All the days ordained for me were written in your book before one of them came to be.

Psalm 139:13-16

It might be easy to remember the story of your early years and forget that God was present all that time. That His plans for your life and mine had already swung into action. In the margin, read the strong word of God in Psalm 139.

List three things you are thankful God knit together in you.

1. _____

2. _____

3. _____

Let's move on to junior high and high school. Did you feel noticed socially? ❧ ❑ yes ❑ no ❧ If so, what memories do you have of being seen and enjoyed by your family, a friend, or a teacher?

_____

_____

_____

Did anyone notice your strengths or passions and affirm the gifts they saw in you? ❧ ❑ yes ❑ no ❧ If so, who was it?

_____

_____

What did he or she say? _____

_____

_____

_____

How did affirmation make you feel? _____

_____

_____

Did you have boyfriends, or did you just write the names of boys on your notebooks? Who were they? _____

_____

_____

What made those guys attractive to you?

_____

_____

_____

_____

The spring of my senior year in high school I discovered contact lenses, got my braces off, and tried a Farrah Fawcett haircut—all within a week or so. I was completely changed on the outside. Maybe even pretty if you tilted your head and squinted. But the die had already been cast on the inside. By the time I graduated from high school, I was sure I would never be beautiful.

By the end of high school, what die had been cast in your heart and soul with regard to beauty? _____

_____

_____

List 10 adjectives that describe you from the inside out.

_____

_____

_____

_____

Did you include the word *beautiful* in your description? Why or why not? _____

_____

_____

> *Angela, I am really struggling with remembering my story. From my earliest memories I have been called beautiful. I remember at the age of four being told I was pretty just before I was molested. In the next years, they always said the same things just before they grabbed me and raped me. I never wanted to be beautiful anymore.*
>
> —Erin

Many in our parents' generation were very pragmatic. Things of beauty were not so highly valued or pursued. There wasn't any time for all the fuss and bother. Eyes down. Work hard. Play little.

Were you affected by a lack of beauty or appreciation of beauty in your growing years? ❑ yes ❑ no If yes, explain.

_____

_____

_____

My friend, a principal at an elementary school, asked 45 female teachers to list 25 of their best attributes. When all were finished, she asked them to raise their hands if one of the attributes they listed was *beautiful.* Not one hand went up. Not a woman in the room felt she had permission to call herself beautiful.

Maybe you've felt the same as those women. *Beautiful* just never crossed your mind. It's not a word you hear very much. Or, maybe it feels as if *beautiful* always belongs to someone else. Things are about to change. You are getting ready to hear the voice of God's love in ways you may have never heard before. God calls you beautiful and it's true.

One day down, more of God's soul work tomorrow. Press on, dear one.

God calls you beautiful and it's true.

GROOVIN' FROM
THE EDGE

You know the whole Cinderella story front to back. You love the part where the glass slipper fits, just as I do. Let your mind wander back to the ball with the prince who's looking for a bride, the evil stepmother and the equally evil stepsisters, the fairy godmother, the mice who make the dress, the whole fairy tale.

> Imagine yourself as one of the characters. Which one would you like to be and why? _____
> _____
> _____

You may have had "Cinderella moments" when you felt noticed and called out. Was it prom night or your wedding or some other special occasion?

> Remember and list as many "Cinderella moments" as you can.
> _____
> _____
> _____

I have a friend who said she had always thought of herself as the fairy godmother. I hadn't even considered her as one of the options. My friend believed that the fun role would be granting everyone's heart desire. I had always thought the whole point was being the girl who was asked to dance.

I always wanted to be Cinderella, but too many junior high lessons kept me from believing I could. I would end up thinking of myself as one of the girls from the kingdom. You know, just one of the girls invited to the ball. She had done the best she could with hair, make-up, and the dress. She was going that evening with all the other hopeful girls from the kingdom. Hoping to be noticed by the prince. Hoping he would be taken by her presence and her laughter. But the girls from the kingdom were never asked to dance.

Can you just see the girls from the kingdom on their way home after the ball? Each one hoped to be noticed by the prince. I'm guessing that on the way home, they were making things up, *That prince was so short, I bet her toes were pinching in those glass slippers,* anything to pretend it really didn't matter that the prince hadn't seen them … or asked them to dance. Pretending they didn't care to cover the pain each one felt.

I think I learned how to pretend in junior high.

How about you and pretending? Did you cover your heartache, pretending you were tough or being noticed didn't matter? Are you pretending now?

List the things you pretend don't matter to you (but really do).

I pretend it doesn't hurt my feelings when _____
_____

I pretend I don't want to _____

I pretend I can't live without _____

Maybe there were a few Cinderella moments for you, but they never quite worked out. Maybe you danced, but no one ever came looking for you later. Maybe the glass slipper fit, but the happily ever didn't come after. Maybe you learned to pretend it didn't matter.

God made you feminine, wired with the desire to be seen and known and loved deeply. He made you with a feminine heart and feminine longings. He is completely aware of His design in you. We were made to be seen and loved and called beautiful. We do not have to hide our hearts from God or pretend we're OK when life actually hurts. Read these words from Psalm 139. Let's make this our memory verse this week.

O LORD, you have searched me
    and you know me.
You know when I sit and when I rise;
    you perceive my thoughts from afar.
You discern my going out and my lying down;
    you are familiar with all my ways.
(vv. 1-3, NIV, emphasis mine)

It's OK to want what you were made for. It's OK to want to be Cinderella, the fairy godmother, or the mice who make the dress.

Are you feeling some hesitancy when I tell you these longings are OK and encouraged in your feminine soul? ❏ yes ❏ no
What makes you hesitant? _____
_____
_____

When my life fell apart in my divorce, I mistakenly thought that my brokenness must make me very ugly to God. Along the way, I let so many factors shape my heart and then on top of everything, I learned to pretend instead of really live. (Besides, most of the women I knew were pretending, too.) When I felt rejection as a teen, I pretended I was OK. When life was disappointing, I pretended in order to cover the pain. For years I pretended to my friends, to my family, and most heart-breaking, to God. I imagined that my broken life made me ugly to God when deep inside all I wanted was to be beautiful to Him.

You see, our life experiences can shape our view of God. We can begin to think things like:

- *No one else notices me, so God probably doesn't either.*
- *The beautiful awards always went to someone else, so those must be the ones who are beautiful to God.*
- *Very few have ever wanted to know my heart or cared about my dreams; maybe God is like all the others.*
- *People would laugh if they knew I longed to be seen and cared for. I'll keep that hidden from God too.*
- *Only silly girls want to be Cinderella. I am a thinking woman and thinking women don't have time for such nonsense.*

How have your own experiences, or even your pretending, mis-shaped your view of God or the truth of your own longings?

_____

_____

Have you ever felt unloved or misunderstood and assumed that God must distance Himself from you too? _____

_____

Pretending is not really living. It makes you feel crazy, and it causes you to believe dumb things about the love of God. Eventually there was a day when it was just me before the Lord—my pain, my insecurity, my deep disappointment about the way life had turned out. I was crying; actually, I was sobbing like a baby. My heart was racing and my chest felt like it was going to explode. And finally, through a blur of tears, these words made their way into my journal:

Oh God, do You think I'm beautiful?

Are You the One who longs for me—the One who can fill this desire to be known? There is so much more inside of me, a great well of passion and dreams. A place I never let myself go. Is it safe to trust You with the rest of my heart? What will You do with me if I show You everything? Every desire? Every longing? Every doubt? Every weakness? If I am exposed before You, will You still love me? Is Your forgiveness truly irreversible? Is Your grace really free? Will You hold me and care for me in the dark?

Oh God, please hold me and tell me that You love me. Tell me I am desirable. Tell me You'll fight for me. Tell me I am beautiful.

I once thought that the words I wrote in my journal that night were intensely personal, but now I know they were intensely feminine. Every woman longs to know from the deepest place of her heart, "Oh God, do You think I'm beautiful?"

We can spend our lives hoping someone will find us beautiful, smart, funny, and worthy of great love. Then we can find ourselves disappointed that no one ever really comes through. We may wind up pretending it really doesn't matter. It turns out that the longing to be called beautiful was put there by God. And He is the only One who can ever give you the answer.

The night I cried my heart out to God, He came with an answer that has changed me forever. I begged to know, "Do you think I'm beautiful?" and in the wilderness of that room, I heard Him say,

"Yes. Your desire has served its purpose, you have finally brought your true heart to Me. Are you tired of the weight of pretending? Are you tired of hoping that someone else will fill the place that was meant for Me? I see you, all of you, and you do not have to hide anymore. I see your sin and your flaws, and I still desire you as My own. I am wildly in love with you. I am the answer for your longing. The 'more' that your heart waits for is Me.

Yes, dear one, yes, you were beautiful to Me before you ever were. Nothing, absolutely nothing, about My love has changed. You are incredibly beautiful to Me."

That night God took me to a passage of Scripture to reveal the heart of His answer.

The king is enthralled by your beauty (Psalm 45:11).

Today, God speaks the truth of those words to you.

Some women live an entire lifetime, die, and go to heaven pretending and smiling politely. I can barely stand the thought of it. I am thankful that one day it finally all came undone for me. Every prop was knocked down. Every place to hide revealed. For the first time, my soul was ripped open and the truth came pouring out. Alone and empty, my heart begged to know, "Oh God, do You think I'm beautiful?"

Now it's your turn. Dog-ear this page. You're going to come back here. Write a prayer below. Ask God if He thinks you're beautiful and boldly request an answer. Date your prayer when you're done. Ask God to be loud and lavish when He answers. Ask Him to speak to you in ways that are unmistakably His.

Your job is to pray and then listen for God's answer. When He answers—and He will—come back here and record what He says.

The question, "Do you think I'm beautiful?" is *really* yours to ask. God wants you to ask Him and then hear what He has to say about you.

The question, "Do you think I'm beautiful?" is really yours to ask. God wants you to ask Him and then hear what He has to say about you.

My Prayer: _____

_____

_____

_____

_____

Date: _____

God's Answer: _____

_____

_____

_____

_____

Date: _____

D A Y   3

THE POWER OF THE QUESTION

God designed the woman inside you. He made her to long for passion, romance, and love. She came with a set of gifts and talents that looks like no other. She was made for beauty and to long to be known as beautiful. She has gotten lost somewhere in the journey of life. I want you to become reacquainted with the woman God thought of when He thought of you.

It may be easier for you to believe this question belongs to every other woman, but it came attached to your soul. God wants you to ask Him because He loves to answer. "The king is enthralled by your beauty" (Psalm 45:11).

Look up Zephaniah 3:17 in your Bible.

Who is the Lord with? _____

Who will He save? _____

In whom does He delight? _____

I imagine God has been trying to speak into your heart for a very long time, but maybe you are just beginning to wake up to His great joy over you. Could you learn to believe that God likes you and wants to pamper you? Maybe you have intellectual knowledge. You believe the Bible verse in your head. To make the transfer from your head to your heart is a work of the Holy Spirit.

Ask God to help you, by the power of the Holy Spirit, begin to believe in your heart that God is captivated by your beauty.

God is captivated by your beauty.

What does Psalm 51:6 suggest to you about God's view of pretending?_____
_____
_____

We can become pleasers just to find some sense of acceptance. When the props fall away, we're left with ourselves. I did not have any idea who I was or what my true heart desired. I didn't know if I liked jazz music more than pop or vice versa. I liked whatever was going to please most of the people in the room. I still don't have all the answers, but I am learning to embrace the truth of my likes and my longings.

It's time to do a little heart work. These questions are tough, so you may have to come back to this section several times after some thought and prayer. Ask God to amaze you with the beauty of your true heart.

Who are you really? _____
_____
_____

What do you like? _____
_____
_____

What do you long for? _____
_____
_____

You may find you have shut down to the things you wanted or what you dreamed of doing with your life. You could remain shut down and numb for the rest of your days. Is God calling your soul awake? Could He be shouting the truth of His devotion to you, hoping this time you're going to hear Him?

Don't skip over this. This is about you. Just you. What do you like? What would you choose to do with your life if it didn't matter what anyone else said or thought? Try to answer from your true heart.

> When do you think you shine? Be honest. What is your absolute best thing? _____
> _____
> _____
>
> Do you feel you can make up your mind on your own, or do you look to someone else to validate your thoughts? Why?
> _____
> _____

Many of us need to find out who we really are and who we want to be. Somewhere in there we will find the woman God lovingly crafted. We can learn to celebrate both her and the lavish love of God.

If there is one thing I want you to get from today's study it is permission to ask, "Do you think I'm beautiful?" I know how hard this is. We aren't supposed to ask this stuff out loud.

It probably feels easier to close the book and not think about it. But don't do that yet. You might keep living the same way you've been living for another 30 years if you don't at least try. Let's keep trying together.

> Make a list of words that describe the beautiful woman you long to be.
> _____
> _____
> _____
>
> Stop now and pray, asking God to wake you up, renew your mind, speak to your doubts, and give you understanding. Ask Him to do an incredible life work in these weeks. Ask Him to make you the woman you described above.

I sought the LORD,
and He heard me,
And delivered me
from all my fears.
They looked to Him
and were radiant,
And their faces were
not ashamed.

Psalm 34:4-5, NKJV

Yesterday my kids had the day off from school. The local skating rink opened for a special afternoon session with a discounted rate for our school. I paid $19.00 for all of us to skate and some of us to have roller blades.

We were the first ones there, so we quickly traded in our shoes and hurried out to the huge wooden floor. A little time passed, but no one else showed up.

At first the kids were whining about wanting other kids to come, but eventually they realized it was pretty cool to have an entire skating rink to ourselves, complete with concession stand and yell-to-the-DJ special requests.

The manager was obviously losing money, but he was great to our family. He cranked up the fog machine, played all the crazy games, worked the multicolored lights and mirrored ball, and played our favorite songs. We danced and raced around that rink for a solid two hours without another soul in sight.

The kids ended up with blisters and my legs were rubber, but, wow, did we have a blast. It was so much fun, we almost forgot anything was wrong with the world. My four kids were holding hands, skating in a line together, forgetting they were siblings. It was the best gift right in the middle of our crazy week. We all left with big smiles plastered to our faces.

Many years have passed since I was the high-school wallflower who was asked to dance, but the experience at the skating rink reminded me what it felt like. I was dancing on wheels with the people I love most in the world. We were singing as loud as we could to our favorite music. No one was standing in the shadows, afraid to try. Each of us was completely given over to joy, the pure pleasure of celebration, the great delight of dancing just because we're alive.

I imagine God smiled as He watched us enjoying His gift—a private skating party for five. God, thank You for the stuff we don't deserve, the surprises that renew our hearts, and the blessing of dancing with the ones we love.

Today's study is about being seen across the room of heaven and earth. God calls you by name and asks you to dance the dance of your life in His arms. It's about what happens when a woman gets that close to God, the place where she is safe and vulnerable and free to ask anything her soul longs to know.

> He does not take his
>   eyes off the righteous;
> he enthrones them
>   with kings
>   and exalts them forever.
>
> Job 36:7

Do you believe what God says about you? Take this quiz to find out. Answer each question T for true or F for false.

_____ 1. I feel God is irritated with me most of the time.
_____ 2. I think God cares about the big picture, but not every detail or problem in my life.
_____ 3. I've sinned too much for God to let me start over.
_____ 4. When God looks at me, He sees what others see.
_____ 5. God knows all about me and loves me anyway.
_____ 6. God wants to be close to me.
_____ 7. God thinks I'm beautiful.
_____ 8. God wants good things for me.
_____ 9. God doesn't understand all I have to deal with.
_____ 10. God really listens when I pray.

Following are the answers. Don't take them from me. Take them from God's Word.

1. False. We do fail and God cares about our failings, but He would rather you try to please Him, even if you fall along the way. Read about David—a man who failed and whom God loved.

2. False. God does care about the big picture, but He also wants to be involved in every detail of your life. He wants to rescue you from pain, in the same way a princess would be rescued by her knight. He even knows how many hairs are on your head. Read Psalm 18:16-19 and Matthew 10:29-31.

3. False. God is willing to forgive you every time you sincerely call for Him. But He is God, the One who cares for your soul, and He desires that you turn away from bad choices. Read Psalm 51 and 1 John 1:9.

4. False. God sees you more completely than any human being can. He created you and He cares about you—inside and out!

5. True. Read Psalm 139.

6. True. You exist to have a relationship with God and enjoy Him forever!

7. True. Read Psalm 45:10-11.

8. True. God wants joy for you. Read Jeremiah 29:11 and Matthew 7:7-12.

9. False. Jesus knows what it feels like to be ignored, lied about, made fun of, betrayed, spit on, misunderstood by His family, and abandoned by His friends. See the gospel books (Matthew, Mark, Luke, John) for the full story.

10. True. It's woven all through the Bible. Read specifically Psalm 145:18.

> Do you remember our memory verse for this week (p. 8)? Rewrite it here and substitute your name every time you can. _____
> _____
> _____
> _____
> _____

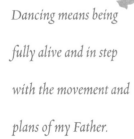

DAY 4

INSIDE HIS ARMS

Dancing means being fully alive and in step with the movement and plans of my Father.

Dancing, for me, is a metaphor for living in the fullness of my gifts and passions. Drinking deeply of relationships, adventure, and learning. Dancing means being fully alive and in step with the movement and plans of my Father. I don't want to miss anything God has for me. I want to grow and become and change. I call it dancing in His arms.

Sometimes I wondered if the wallflower role was my calling in life, always watching and never truly entering in. I felt my feet wanted to, but I'd say to myself, "Nah, quit dreaming about dancing and go make dinner."

How would you fill in this blank?

Quit dreaming about _____ and go make dinner.

I am hoping you just wrote the truth of your longing, that thing inside you that sets off the passion siren. Have you heard the shrieks of your passion lately? Or have they been silenced by the weight of your life? the spin of your family? the time already passed?

The God of heaven is speaking your name. He is calling your passions alive. He is inviting you into the romance of His love. I imagine that as you are working through this study, God is beginning to stir something inside you.

> How are you hearing God call your name? How is God calling your
> soul awake? Journal about these stirrings.
>
> _____
> _____
> _____
> _____
> _____

One author says there are seven longings of the human heart that do not need to be repented of. He believes that we came with these longings and they will either be met in God and in relationships He provides, or we'll find a way to meet those longings outside His provision in sin.[2]

> Read the list of longings below. Do you see these desires behind
> the way you live your own life, or have you tried to deny their
> existence or importance? Journal your thoughts about each one.
>
> 1. The longing for assurance that we are loved. _____
> _____
> _____
>
> 2. The longing for enjoyment. _____
> _____
> _____
>
> 3. The longing to be beautiful. _____
> _____
> _____
>
> 4. The longing to be great. _____
> _____
> _____

5. The longing for intimacy without shame. _____

_____

_____

6. The longing to be wholehearted and passionate. _____

_____

_____

7. The longing to make a deep and lasting impact. _____

_____

_____

For many of us, when we first consider our longings, nothing comes to mind. That can tell us we've shut down our hearts in the effort to make life hurt less. As we keep pursuing God about this, He will help us recognize who we really are called to be. God wants us to desire a significant life. He wired us to long for beauty.

Is there a passion that stands in the shadows of your life? Something inside you that longs to dance again or for the very first time? A yearning that was built into your design, placed there by God? Ask Him to show you specifically what you long for and where you have been hindered or how your heart has shut down. Ask Him to release you into a passionate life.

Or, if you know what you are passionate about, what needs to happen for you to give yourself permission to dream about your longings again? Do you need the man you love to give you wings? Do you need someone to believe in you? Ask friends to pray about this with you. Come back to this page and these thoughts. He will take you deeper as you press into Him.

Listen, O daughter,
  consider and give ear:
Forget your people and
  your father's house.
The king is enthralled
  by your beauty;
honor him, for he
  is your lord.

Psalm 45:10-11

Read Psalm 45:10–11 in the margin. Rewrite those verses here, substituting your name wherever possible.

_____

_____

_____

_____

_____

Enthralled means "captivated, smitten, fascinated, spellbound, and delighted." Enthralled is how God feels about you. How does your heart respond to that?

_____

_____

_____

_____

Do you hesitate when you hear these ideas? ✍ ❑ yes ❑ no ✍
If so, what holds you back? _____

_____

_____

_____

Romance. Passion. Dancing. These aren't the words we usually use to describe our relationship with God. But do they ring true with your soul? When you are brutally honest with yourself, doesn't your heart long for passion?

Maybe the thoughts of romance were ruined for you years ago. An awful relationship or marriage. Terrible childhood memories of molestation or worse. Do you know God never intended romance to be ugly? His creation of this kind of intimacy is pure and without pain.

If you need to, ask God right now to begin changing the ideas you associate with romance. Give Him your hesitancy and fears.

Romance and passion are incredibly beautiful gifts the Father gave us. And the longing to be known intimately is a desire that came attached to the soul. We don't have to be ashamed for longing to be held and loved. It's OK to want that for which we were made.

D A Y   5

THE GOD THING

One day a friend asked me, "Angela, why does all this have to be about the God thing?" Even though we don't all voice it, the truth of the question is incredibly real to most of us. Either we still wrestle with our understanding of God or someone around us questions why it has to be about Him.

Very little in this study is going to make sense if you haven't nailed down what you believe about the reality of God. There are many dimensions to this amazing God of ours, but I want us to review a few of His names and attributes before we go any further.

GOD, THE CREATOR

The whole idea of *you* came from God the Creator. God dreamed you before you ever were. He fashioned you in the image of one He adores.

You created my inmost being;
   you knit me together in my mother's womb.
I praise you because I am fearfully and wonderfully made;
   your works are wonderful, I know that full well.
My frame was not hidden from you
   when I was made in the secret place.
When I was woven together in the depths of the earth,
   your eyes saw my unformed body.
All the days ordained for me
   were written in your book
   before one of them came to be.

Psalm 139:13-16

Journal your praise or thoughts about God as our Creator.

_____

_____

_____

_____

_____

_____

GOD, THE FATHER

In the Gospels, Jesus uses the word *Abba* to refer to God. Literally translated, *Abba* means "daddy." In our great and awesome God abides the heart of a Father … Daddy. We can come to Him knowing He cares for us and interacts with us with all the compassion and tenderness of a daddy who fusses over his beautiful daughter. Maybe your earthly dad never acted like he was smitten or taken with you. Do not let this tarnish the truth of your Daddy in heaven—our God who longs to hold you in the arms of His strength and provision. Let's look for a moment at what Scripture says about the Father.

Jesus said His miracles came from the Father. *"I have shown you many great miracles from the Father. For which of these do you stone me?" (John 10:32).*

Jesus only does what the Father instructs Him to do. *"When you have lifted up the Son of Man, then you will know that I am the one I claim to be and that I do nothing on my own but speak just what the Father has taught me" (John 8:28).*

No one can snatch you out of the Father's hand. *"My Father, who has given them to me, is greater than all; no one can snatch them out of my Father's hand" (John 10:29).*

The Father gives grace and peace. *"Grace and peace to you from God our Father and the Lord Jesus Christ" (Ephesians 1:2).*

Every good and perfect gift comes to us from the Father. *"Every good and perfect gift is from above, coming down from the Father of the heavenly lights, who does not change like shifting shadows" (James 1:17).*

God is a father to the fatherless. *"A father to the fatherless, a defender of widows, is God in his holy dwelling" (Psalm 68:5).*

Do you have anything you'd like to say to your Father? Do you need to hear His tender voice of direction and sense that He loves you like a daddy? Linger with your thoughts about our God who loves you with the heart of a father. What is He saying to you?

GOD, THE SON, OUR SAVIOR

God came as Jesus Christ, the Son, to be our Savior. Knowing that His created ones would never be able to save themselves from the consequences of sin, God, in His mercy, came as Jesus to live, teach, train, and die as punishment for the sins of the world. You and I are separated from the holiness of God by our sin. The death and resurrection of Jesus made a way for you and me to cross over into fellowship with our Almighty God. God says that when we believe Jesus Christ is His Son and His death can cover our sins, then we can be saved from punishment.

I had known about Jesus all my life. When I finally came to understand that Jesus died on the cross to pay for my sin, I prayed to God and asked Him to be my Savior. But I wasn't certain, so I did the whole thing again. Then I wondered if I prayed the right words, so I prayed again with different words. I bet I asked God to save me at least 150 times over several years. I just could not find an assurance that I had done everything perfectly.

A time finally came when I was again in front of God, asking Him to save me. I said, "God, if there is something else I need to do to be saved, don't hide it from me. I want You. I want Your forgiveness. I want to spend eternity with You. Show me if I've missed something." I seemed to hear in my head, "Enough already. I have not hidden Myself from you. You are saved forever." It's been completely settled in my heart ever since.

> Most of us came to understand God as the Son and our Savior at some particular point in our lives. What is your story? When did you first understand Jesus as the Savior?
>
> _____
>
> _____
>
> _____
>
> _____
>
> _____

Maybe you haven't ever nailed down your belief about Jesus. If you haven't ever prayed and asked Jesus to forgive you of your sins and be your Savior, you can do that right now. Use your own words and talk to God about your desire. You'll want to remember the day you turned your life over to God, so journal your prayer on a separate sheet of paper or in a notebook and date it. Then tell someone else who loves God about your prayer. They will want to rejoice with you and walk with you as you begin to learn more about God, our Savior.

GOD, THE HOLY SPIRIT

The Holy Spirit is God who comes to live in our souls when we ask God the Son to save us. The Holy Spirit is the presence of God who gives us guidance and discernment. He reveals the sin in our lives. And He intercedes for us before the throne of God.

If we keep to the dance analogy, we might say the Holy Spirit is the Person who invites us into the arms of God. He is the voice we sense calling us into this very intimate and personal relationship.

In the Book of John, Jesus promised that He would send the Holy Spirit to help us: "I will pray the Father, and He will give you another Helper, that He may abide with you forever—the Spirit of truth, whom the world cannot receive, because it neither sees Him nor knows Him; but you know Him, for He dwells with you and will be in you" (John 14:16-17, NKJV).

> How do you know when the Holy Spirit is giving you direction?
>
> _____
>
> _____

> Ask some of your close friends in Christ how they know when the Holy Spirit is prompting their thoughts or actions.

GOD IS LOVE

What we have come to call love, the yearning inside each of us to be enjoyed by someone else and to give that same joy in return, is the very nature of God.

> Look up 1 John 4:7-18 and answer these brief questions.
> Where does love come from (v. 7)?_____
>
> According to verse 15, what happens to the person who acknowledges that Jesus is the Son of God? _____
> _____
>
> What does the love of God do in our lives (vv. 12,17)?
> _____
> _____

Lest you begin to believe that the great love of God is for everyone except you, read Ephesians 2:4-8. God wants you to understand it is His incomprehensible love that allows Him to love sinful people—people like you and me. Love for the unlovable, the disobedient, the wayward, the scarred. It's called *grace*.

> Immense in mercy and with an incredible love, he embraced us. He took our sin-dead lives and made us alive in Christ. He did all this on his own, with no help from us! Then he picked us up and set us down in highest heaven …
>
> Now God has us where he wants us, with all the time in this world and the next to shower grace and kindness upon us in Christ Jesus. Saving is all his idea, and all his work. All we do is trust him enough to let him do it. It's God's gift from start to finish! We don't play the major role. If we did, we'd probably go around bragging that we'd done the whole thing! No, we neither make nor save ourselves. God does both the making and saving.
>
> *Ephesians 2:4-10, The Message*

This love is from God. His amazing, gracious, and completing love is meant for you. You and I are invited to dance in His arms just because of His mercy and grace. No previous experience required. Free dancing lessons to everyone who would believe He is True. Come one, come all. The music has already started. Just follow His lead.

You and I are invited to dance in His arms just because of His mercy and grace. No previous experience required. Free dancing lessons to everyone who would believe He is True. The music has already started. Just follow His lead.

---

1. Angela Thomas, *Do You Think I'm Beautiful?* (Nashville: Thomas Nelson, 2003), 1-2.

2. Mike Bickle, "The Holy Passion of the Bride," *Charisma*, March 1999, 92-96.

When the Wallflower
Is Asked to Dance

WEEK 2

If there is a question attached to the soul of a woman, maybe it's, "Do you think I'm beautiful?" When God answers from the depth of His great love, it makes some of us feel like the wallflower who is asked to dance.

Did you see the movie *My Big Fat Greek Wedding?* Everything was so over-the-top. The passion. The love. The dancing. The food. The hair. Every part of their lives was huge and wild with emotion … almost out of control. After I saw the movie, I left the theater feeling like the vanilla in-laws and wishing I were Greek. I left feeling as if everything fun in life is outside my box. All the lines I had drawn around my life seemed to leave the passion out. Then one day my friend said to me, "What if God is Greek too?"

I can't tell you how much hope that gave me. What if God kissed you as though He'd known you forever? What if He yelled with delight every time He saw you? What if God had never known a stranger, His table was always overflowing, and everyone was family? What if He was full of emotion concerning every bit of your life? What if lots of dancing, celebration, and laughter were present whenever you were with God? I think that has to be how God is. I'd love to be in the middle of all that love. Even better, I'd love to give away wild and passionate love like that.

"Whoever touches you touches the apple of his eye" (Zechariah 2:8).

VIEWER GUIDE

"Long before he laid down earth's foundations, he had us in mind,
had settled on us as the focus of his love, to be made whole and
holy by his love. ... (What pleasure he took in planning this!)"
Ephesians 1:4-5, THE MESSAGE

The Lord created us with an _____ _____ inside only He can fill.

No _____ can do what the Savior is supposed to do in your life.

You can still be made whole even if your _____ _____ didn't give you what he should have.

Your _____ can never fill you up and make you whole.

_____ can't ever be enough to be the Savior your empty place needs.

New _____ doesn't even give you a taste of being filled by God.

The only way is the _____ way!

GOD ANSWERS OUR QUESTIONS

DO YOU NOTICE ME?

Memory Verse

Then the woman, seeing that she could not go unnoticed, came trembling and fell at his feet.

Luke 8:47

Maybe you still feel like the wallflower. Maybe you still can't imagine God walking across the room to speak your name. Maybe you can't believe you have been seen and adored. Has God allowed you to live many years in wallflowerdom so that in these moments He could shatter that image with powerful authority? Does He want you to realize that being a wallflower is not the life He planned for you? Do you want to believe God has more for you?

What holds you back from believing there is more?

_____

_____

_____

_____

_____

Recount a time when you felt wonderfully noticed.

_____

_____

_____

If you make the Most High your dwelling—
   even the LORD, who
   is my refuge—
then no harm will
   befall you,
no disaster will come near
   your tent.
For he will command his
   angels concerning
   you to guard you
   in all your ways.

Psalm 91:9-11

Read Psalm 91:9-11 (margin). What is the condition in this passage? (Hint: the words that come after "If.") _____

_____

What are the promises for those who make God their dwelling?

_____

How does it feel to know that God appoints angels to guard your coming and going (Psalm 91:11), your waking and sleeping? Our God does not sleep. His eyes are continually upon you. Nothing about your life goes unseen.

Sometimes my children will ask, "Mama, why are you staring at me?" It's just because I love to watch them do what they do. I love to quietly watch AnnaGrace play and talk with her dolls. I enjoy watching Grayson show

William how to build a Lego man. I love to watch them because they are mine. Even more, our God delights in noticing His created.

Ask God to be unmistakable in letting you know He sees and notices you. Ask Him very specifically and then date your prayer. Come back to this place when you have seen or heard His answer. Record and date what you have received from God. Let us not forget the great works of God in our own lives. He truly does answer our prayers.

My Prayer: _____
_____
_____
_____
_____

Date: _____

God's Answer: _____
_____
_____
_____
_____

Date: _____

IS ANYONE LISTENING TO ME?

When was the last time you felt unheard? This morning with your kids? Last night with your husband? This week at work? With a friend? A neighbor? Another family member?

_____
_____
_____

Read Psalm 34:17 and ask God to hear your prayers and answer your cries to be heard. Do you want someone safe to talk to? Ask God for provision. Do you need counseling you cannot afford? Ask God. Do you long for the ears of your children? Come before the Lord and ask Him to make it so. What do you need? Write it out. He is waiting to hear.

_____
_____
_____
_____

Is anyone crying for help? GOD is listening, ready to rescue you.

Psalm 34:17, THE MESSAGE

Women ache for intimate connection. A desperate loneliness settles on the heart not heard. Lonely for companionship. Lonely for expression. Lonely for affirmation.

WILL YOU RESCUE ME?

This question may be tough for you. As you look over the events of your life, you may have heard yourself ask it somewhere in your past. There may be pain associated with remembering.

Has there been a time when you needed to be rescued but felt abandoned by God? ❧ ❏ yes ❏ no ❧ Ask God where He was during the event you are remembering. This may feel intense for you. The answer may not come immediately, and you may want to walk through these prayers with a counselor or friend.

_____

_____

_____

_____

_____

_____

_____

_____

When you did not feel the Lord rescue, what conclusions did you draw about yourself?

❏ I'm not worth saving.   ❏ I deserved it.

❏ I caused it.   ❏ I was made to be used.

❏ I was being punished for previous sin.

Remembering a painful past and asking God for His answers may be incredibly difficult. Read this answer for our question from Scripture.

> Watch this: God's eye is on those who respect him,
> the ones who are looking for his love.
> He's ready to come to their rescue in bad times;
> in lean times he keeps body and soul together.
>
> *Psalm 33:18-19, The Message*

God is a rescuing God. He can begin healing your past. Maybe you need to be rescued from a season or place in your life. Maybe you need to be rescued from a relationship. Maybe you need to be rescued from your own choices and bad habits. Come to God with the truth of your need.

DO YOU REALLY LOVE ME?

If we want anything in this lifetime, it's deep, unfailing love. Some of us have tasted it and want more. Some of us have never known it and yet desire it intensely. And some of us have long ago given up on really being loved. For me, the question "Do you really love me?" means:

> *Will you accept me in process? Will you embrace what is different about me and applaud my efforts to become? Can I just be human—strong and vibrant some days, weak and frail others? Can I have a relationship with you without pretending? Can I be honest and expect honesty? Is it OK if my hair looks gross, my morning breath is not minty fresh, and my jeans are stretched around a few extra pounds? Will you love me even if I disappoint you? Will you love me through dark places? Will you love me even when I doubt your love?*

Think about the people in your life. What does the question "Do you really love me?" mean to you?

_____

_____

_____

_____

Have you heard God tell you that He loves you lately?
❏ yes ❏ no   If yes:

How? _____

_____

_____

When? _____

_____

Where?_____

_____

You and I were made with an empty place that can be filled only by the unfailing love of God. What is going on in your life that keeps His love from being enough for you?

_____

_____

_____

_____

_____

"God, do You really see me in all this mess and still call me beautiful? Even when my breath is not minty-fresh and my hair looks gross? Do You really love me in spite of my flaws?"

And God replies ...

"If you could only grasp how wide and how high and how deep, then you'd know, I really love you."

What a man desires is unfailing love.

Proverbs 19:22

33

Sometimes we can lose our way and forget our design. Maybe we need to ask God to give us a craving for His love. A fresh desire for His filling. A yearning for the fullness that can come only from Him. Pray and ask God to make you hungry for Him.

> Do you have other questions for God regarding your hopes and dreams for love? Write them in your own words as honestly as you would speak them to a friend. _____
>
> _____
>
> _____
>
> _____
>
> _____

GO AHEAD AND DANCE

We've been talking about dancing, wallflowers, and God. I have told you that God sees you across the room and thinks you are incredibly beautiful. He is inviting you to dance in His arms. It's safe there, and you can whisper into His ear all the questions your heart longs to ask. This dance is the dance of your life. The one He envisioned when He dreamed of you.

These are big truths that could impact the way you face life every day. What kind of woman would you be if you believed this stuff? What kind of life could you have if you were truly dancing? The God of heaven is looking at you, watching you stand around the edge of your life. And He is asking you to dance. What are you going to do?

My friend prayed something like this:

David ... danced with great abandon before GOD.

2 Samuel 6:14, THE MESSAGE

> *Lord, I am standing up against the wall in the shadows, and I am scared. I don't really know people who dance. Nobody in my family dances. Most of the people I know are afraid to go for it. They seem afraid to really trust You to lead. Maybe they are afraid they'll look like fools.*
>
> *I want to dance with You. Are You giving me permission to move toward the things I've been trying to hide from all my life? My desire to be pretty? My longing to dream big dreams? My feet that want to dance and run through life with joy? God, if You're asking me to dance, I don't ever want to forget it. Would You please ask me to dance in such a way that I know it's You? I do love You, God, and I love knowing You see me over here hiding. Amen.*

I feel the most beautiful when _____

_____

When I think of God being totally in love with me, I feel _____

_____

Knowing that God loves me, flaws and all, makes me want to

_____

_____

D A Y   2

THE OTHER LOVERS

Today is Valentine's Day. The day everybody wants to be loved by somebody. The desire to be desired by someone you desire. That craving for love wired into our souls. Today is all about the other lovers in our lives. A celebration of romance. Dreamy cards. Long-stemmed roses. Candlelight dinners. Chocolate hearts. Whispered passion. Lingering looks. And of course, dancing.

I ran three errands this morning, and, boy, is love in the air! They were hauling roses by the truckload into a kiosk at the mall. Mylar balloons were tied to every store fixture, each boasting a bigger and brighter way to say, "I love you." At the drugstore, person after person stood in line with me to buy cards, candy, and flowers. I had gone for mascara and razors, but all the hoopla sure got me in the mood. The lady who checked me out wore dangling pink-and-red-lips earrings. She said she'd already gotten roses from her husband before she left for work. I told her it sounded as if he loved her. She said, "He'd better." I smiled to myself, figuring that he knew he'd better get her flowers too.

It's the big love day, or is it? It's not even lunchtime, and I've already talked to four people in my life who are mourning this day. One friend is 38 and single. She just wanted to call in sick this morning, skip this day altogether. She said she'll probably get a fruit basket delivered to her door. There will be a sweet card that says, "You are amazing. You are wonderful. We love you, Mom and Dad." Somehow that fruit basket makes the absence of love all the more brilliant. Her heart aches to be desired, and the pain is intense today.

My next girlfriend is married, but her husband hasn't lived at home in a few years. They used to protect this day just for the two of them, a time of intimate and tender celebration. Now she cries through it. She knows he'll be with someone else tonight. Her soul longs for the love that was and aches for the man who is gone.

Gabriel greeted [Mary]: "Good morning! You're beautiful with God's beauty, Beautiful inside and out!"

Luke 1:28, THE MESSAGE

My next friend did everything right. He's got the girl. Made reservations for dinner and dancing at the club. Bought diamond earrings, cards, and roses. But she called and decided not to come. Something about a swim practice. He's devastated. Oh my goodness, how love hurts.

Then there's Carlye. Her son, Rob, died a year ago this day at age 34. She called me from the cemetery where she and Jerry were tending to his flowers. Rob's headstone reads, *Our funny Valentine*. Could there be a pain any greater? I don't think there is.

There's no denying it, especially not today. We were made for relationship. We were made to fall in love and give love and be loved. We were made for the other lovers in our lives, and yet, sometimes, with other love, there is pain.

I'll try to tread softly, because I realize for many of us, this hurts. Our honesty before God will bring truth. The truth of our real needs. The truth of our mistakes. The truth of God's gentle provision. Truth will make a way for healing. And the healing salve of God's love can begin to make you whole again.

I've told everyone else today, and so I'll tell you. I love you. I love that you are diligently seeking the Father's arms. Willing to face the shadows where you have been hiding. I love that you want to dance.

Before we get into the deeper waters, let's splash around with fun memories. Do you remember your first puppy love?
❧ ❑ yes   ❑ no ❧ *What about your first kiss?* ❧ ❑ yes   ❑ no ❧
Does remembering make you smile? ❧ ❑ yes   ❑ no ❧
If so, what is it about that memory that makes you grin?

_____

_____

Can you admit to a continued longing for romance and passion? Or have you labeled your desires as foolish and banished them to a faraway land? ❧ ❑ I have a longing for romance and passion.
❑ Longing for romance and passion is foolish and a waste of my time. ❧

If we are supposed to be dancing in the arms of God and He is supposed to be enough, then why do we have this intense need for others to give us love? What is the role of the other people who love us, the other lovers in our hearts and lives? Why do women spend their lives pining for the affections of men? Why do we hold on to the memories of what we have experienced and the fantasies of what could be? Why does it matter if others notice or call us beautiful? Why did we believe that a man would be the answer?

We want to believe that dancing with God is enough, but we still feel ourselves longing for people. God *is* truly enough, but our lives were never intended to be confined to solitary interaction with God and no one else. We were also made by God to crave the affection of others. We were made for rela-

---

Nothing spoils the taste of peanut butter like unrequited love.

— Charlie Brown

Insert your name in each of the following blanks:

Long before he laid down earth's foundations, he had _____ in mind, had settled on _____ as the focus of his love, to be made whole and holy by his love. Long, long ago he decided to adopt _____ into his family through Jesus Christ. (What pleasure he took in planning this!) He wanted _____ to enter into the celebration of his lavish gift-giving by the hand of his beloved Son.

Ephesians 1:4-6, THE MESSAGE

tionship, for the community of other human beings. It's just that somewhere along the way we hoped someone could make us whole.

It is amazing to finally understand there is an empty place inside of us reserved only for God and then to learn how to give and receive love from His filling of that place—His wholeness. We find ourselves confused and wandering when we try to fill our emptiness apart from God.

Let's run through Theology 101 to track the logic of this thinking:

You and I were made—body, soul, and mind—by _____.
We were made for _____.
The part of us that longs to be filled with love is our _____.
The soul is empty, but can be made whole by _____.

There you go. Made by God, for God, with a soul that can be made whole only by His love (see Ephesians 1:4-5).

These truths are pivotal. We can't really go much further until we get this nailed down. You and I were designed to long for love, and yet the only love that will ever make us whole is the holy love of God. You and I were *made* to be loved by God. We are the object of His affection and the desire of His longings. We've gotten it confused, but God lets us get it right. He can mercifully change the entire course of your life with new understanding about truth.

> He chose us in Him, before the foundation of the world, to be holy and blameless in His sight. In love He predestined us to be adopted through Jesus Christ for Himself, according to His favor and will.
>
> Ephesians 1:4-5, HCSB

Over the course of your life, what have you believed would make you whole? Who or what have you pursued in the hopes of filling your empty places? _____
_____
_____

How have those pursuits turned out? Have you attained a goal or won the heart of a man only to realize it wasn't enough?
_____
_____
_____

Sometimes I still catch myself putting a person or a goal on a pedestal, and I have to take it to God and say something like this:

> *God, I've done it again. I have run after something as though it would fill my soul. Here I am, still empty. Forgive me for chasing the wind. Please take me back into Your arms. Fill my emptiness with Your love. Hold me close. Let me dance with You. Amen.*

You were designed to fall to pieces apart from God's filling. You are supposed to feel frazzled and afraid without His strength. We will succumb to the power of temptation without God's overcoming Spirit. Ask God to continue refilling your soul. Ask Him for the wholeness that comes from His love.

D A Y   3

THE MAN

Healthy love. We are made for it. Want it. Can't get enough of it. *Healthy* is the operative word. Things will forever remain off track and unhealthy if you believe the man you love can, will, or should make you whole.

Read the following traits of healthy and unhealthy relationships.[1] If your significant relationships tend toward the right side of the page, you have probably found yourself in some very miserable patterns of relating. There is a good possibility that one or both of you are expecting the other to give wholeness.

Healthy and Mature	Unhealthy and Immature
1. Allows for individuality because you are free to be yourself.	1. Feels all-consuming with the pressure to please the other.
2. Based on trust—words and actions are expressed consistently and honestly.	2. Based on distrust and fear—feel the need to guard yourself with the other person.
3. Open sharing of feelings. Free and spontaneous.	3. Closed emotionally. Shut down. Controlling; afraid of criticism.
4. Feels free to ask honestly for what is needed and wanted.	4. Plays psychological head games trying to fish for hidden secrets.
5. Serves with passion. Focused and interested.	5. Sense that you are being appeased. Uncertain. Ambivalent.
6. Welcomes closeness and is willing to risk being vulnerable.	6. Fears closeness and sees vulnerability as a threat.

7. Free to enjoy alone time and solitude without partner.	7. Fears abandonment and loneliness.
8. Gives and receives unconditionally.	8. Gives in order to get. Selfish.
9. Maintains other friendships and relationships without a threat.	9. Neglects other friendships and family members out of insecurity.
10. Doesn't attempt to change the other.	10. Attempts to change the other.

If you found your significant relationships plagued with unhealthy traits, I have a few recommendations:

• *Own it.* Label your relationship unhealthy and stop pretending that it's going to fix itself.

• *Talk to God* about the place you're in, the person you love, and your great desire for health. Ask Him for direction and wisdom as you seek healing. Keep asking. Do not be timid with God. Pour it all out and beg Him for power to change.

• *Get help as soon as possible.* Run, don't walk, to the nearest godly counselor and jump in with both feet. Commit yourself to the long journey back toward healthy love.

• *Don't try to do this alone.* Real healing doesn't happen because you shut yourself off from the rest of the world. Healing happens in the context of strong relationships—people who love you and want good things for your life. You need a couple of great friends to jump in with you, keep your confidences, and encourage your efforts.

What practical steps can you take to let the man in your life just be a man? _____

_____

_____

_____

What unrealistic expectations have you had about this man?

_____

_____

_____

_____

How can you be more responsible and mature in your love for him?

_____

_____

_____

THE OTHER MAN

"Like it or not—your father has made a lasting impression on you. Whether he was close or distant, present or absent, cold or warm, loving or abusive, your father has left his mark on you. Your father is still influencing your life today—probably more than you realize." [2]

Much of our identity as women has come through our relationship, or lack of, with the other man in our lives—our fathers.

In what ways do you think you are like your dad?

_____
_____
_____
_____

What traits of your father do you want to avoid in your life?

_____
_____
_____
_____

Has his influence been good or bad, provided strength or weakness? In what ways? _____

_____
_____
_____
_____
_____

Insert your name in the spaces and speak these words to God..

Our Perfect Father

I, _____, believe You are not distant. You are not judgmental toward _____. You do not reject _____. You will never harm _____. You are a good Father who wants good things for _____. You love _____ perfectly.

Our relationship with our fathers also affects our perception of who God is. In *Always Daddy's Girl*, Norman Wright said, "Imagine a little girl of seven who has known only rejection and abuse from her father whom she loves dearly. At Sunday School she is taught that God is her heavenly Father. What is her perception of Him going to be? Based on her experience with her natural father, she will see God as an unstable, rejecting, abusing person she cannot trust." [3]

It is difficult to run into the arms of your Heavenly Father and dance without a good understanding of who He is. If your perception of God has been tainted because of your earthly dad, review the following truths of who God wants to be in your life.

As you read through these characteristics of God outlined by Norman Wright, ask yourself, *Which of these do I need God to be right now?* Highlight those statements and look up the corresponding verses. Make notes in the margin and spend some time in prayer.

He is the loving, concerned Father who is interested in even the intimate details of our lives (Matthew 6:25-34).

He is the Father who never gives up on us (Luke 15:3-32).

He is the God who sent His Son to die for us though we were undeserving (Romans 5:8).

He stands with us in good and bad circumstances (Hebrews 13:5).

He is the ever-active Creator of our universe. He died to heal our sickness, pain and grief (Isaiah 53:3-6).

He has broken the power of death (Luke 24:6-7).

He gives all races and sexes equal status (Galatians 3:28).

He is available to us through prayer (John 14:13-14).

He is aware of our needs (Isaiah 65:24).

He created us for eternal relationship with Him (John 3:16).

He values us (Luke 7:28).

He doesn't condemn us (Romans 8:1).

[He] values and causes our growth (1 Corinthians 3:7).

He comforts us (2 Corinthians 1:3-5).

He strengthens us through His Spirit (Ephesians 3:16).

He cleanses us from sin (Hebrews 10:17-22).

He is for us (Romans 8:31).

He is always available to us (Romans 8:38-39).

He is a God of hope (Romans 15:13).

He helps us in temptation (Hebrews 2:17-18).

He provides a way to escape temptation (1 Corinthians 10:13).

He is at work in us (Philippians 2:13).

He wants us to be free (Galatians 5:1).

He is the Lord of time and eternity (Revelation 1:8).[4]

Your dad is meant to be a vessel of God's love. Maybe he has been that. Maybe he failed miserably. Maybe you have to unlearn everything you have known about fathers so you can come to know the wild-about-you love of your Heavenly Father. Don't let these pages pass in vain. If you have soul work to do in regard to your dad, then stay here longer. Seek the voice of God. Wait until you have heard Him speak into your heart. Walk as He leads. Act as He directs.

DAY 4

MORE OTHER LOVERS

THE CHILDREN

Her children arise and call her blessed.

Proverbs 31:28

I have four little rascals. Two girls and two boys. I'm crazy about them. I think about them and their schedules a lot. I worry about their tender hearts, and I pray for their protection. I could spend most of every day doing or thinking or praying for these four people. I love them so much. Almost every day I tell them how proud I am to be their mama. And I am. Glowing. Beaming. Goofy in love. I see how some of us begin to think that such blessings as our children will fill up the emptiness, that maybe their lives can make us whole. But we must remember Ephesians 1:4-5. Only the love of God can make us whole.

Do you need to release your kids from the responsibility of making your life complete? ❏ yes ❏ no

How can you best set them free? _____

_____

_____

_____

Do they feel pressure to perform or love in certain ways just to please you? ❏ yes ❏ no ❏ I don't think so. How have you laid on the pressure, and what steps can you take to change that?

_____

_____

_____

_____

Have you tried to find your security in their love? ❏ yes ❏ no How can you increase their security, and how can you decrease any insecurity they may battle? _____

_____

_____

_____

They may be great kids, but they cannot fill that empty place inside of you. Only God can do that.

THE FRIENDS

I know a group of women, all in their mid-40s, who have just disbanded as close friends. A part of me asks, "What in the world went wrong? Don't we all know how to be kind and friendly at this point in our lives?" This group of loving women went their separate ways because ultimately one could not find the wholeness and depth she required. Time and time again their trips and get-togethers were plagued by deep disappointment and heartache. They would sit for hours in long discussion, believe they were starting fresh, and then the same issues would resurface.

Most of their pain happened because a few forgot the order. A girlfriend is only a vessel. She can give a part of the love. She can be fun and interesting. But she will come up short, show up late, and misunderstand. She is just a girl. She is just a friend to be treasured. She cannot make you whole.

A friend loves at all times.

Proverbs 17:17

Who in your life would be blessed by a card or a note declaring your friendship? _____

Who needs to know you get a part of God's love from her place in your life? _____

Is there a woman who has felt undue pressure to make you whole?
❧ ❑ yes ❑ no ❧ Is an apology in order? ❧ ❑ yes ❑ no ❧
Does restoration need to happen? ❧ ❑ yes ❑ no ❧
If you answered yes to any of these questions, use the lines below to create a plan for how you will start this process.

_____
_____
_____
_____
_____

Some of the best relationships in my life are those with my girlfriends, but I'd ruin everything if I expected even one of them could make me whole. It's the same song, fourth verse, God made us to be filled by His love. A girlfriend can be fun, but she cannot be your savior. We need God.

THE STUFF

As women, most of us want to surround ourselves with our interpretation of beauty. I heard a man say that when you meet a woman who lacks a touch of beauty in her life, you have met a woman who has been traumatized. I believe he was probably right. It's a part of our nature to want our homes to be lovely and our clothes to reflect our style. I believe that choosing to pursue beauty in our homes or in the way we dress is perfectly wonderful. It's just that when we begin to believe that stuff can fill an emptiness, we've crossed over into unhealthy.

Let's take a few minutes with some of Jesus' words in the Sermon on the Mount. Read Matthew 6:25-33 in your Bible and answer the following questions:

Jesus said not to worry. Specifically, what things did He tell us not to worry about? _____

_____

_____

According to verse 25, what is more important than food, the body, or clothing?_____

_____

What did Jesus say about our value to the Father?_____

_____

Can worrying add anything to our lives (v. 27)? ❧ ❏ yes ❏ no ❧

Does the Father know your needs (v. 32)? ❧ ❏ yes ❏ no ❧

What physical needs do you have? As you are thinking and writing, pray about these needs and take each one to your Father.

_____

_____

_____

_____

_____

What did Jesus command of us in verse 33? _____

_____

In that same verse, what is the promise attached to our obedience?

_____

How could you apply the truths of this passage to your life regarding your stuff?_____

_____

_____

I am struggling with loneliness and fear. I am 33 and have been divorced for two years. I am searching for the romance you spoke so much about from the Lord. I don't feel like I've found that, and I catch myself still looking for it in a man. I've been alone for two years and I have learned more in those desperate times of loneliness and depression than I could ever explain. I think the hardest lesson I've learned is to sit and know that He is God. To sit and be still and patient for His timing and not try to meet my own desperate needs.

—Kristin

RELATIONSHIP NEEDED

The attraction, need, and desire for other intimate relationships in our lives is a very wonderful thing. When spiritual and emotional health exist, these amazing people can touch and transform our lives in powerful ways. God uses these people to heal, restore, and bring great delight into our days.

How do you respond to the idea that women can lust for relationship with the same intensity men can lust for sex?

_____
_____
_____

How have you seen other women make relationships either an idol or an obsession?_____
_____
_____
_____

Describe how women you know have set themselves up for great relationship disappointment. _____
_____
_____
_____

What do you think causes a woman to believe someone or something will make her whole? _____
_____
_____
_____
_____

God is the only Love who can fill your soul.

He is the only One who will ever be enough.

His love promises to make you whole.

The love you have tasted here on Earth through the people in your life is just the beginning, an appetizer, if you will. God has an entire feast of love waiting for you. He will be your fullness and make you whole.

> Before we press on into the heart of God's love for you, write a prayer of thankfulness. Think about each person in your life who gives you a part of the love of God. Each was hand-chosen by God to love you. List each one and thank God for his or her place in your life. Then pray for one specific need you know each has.
>
> _____
> _____
> _____
> _____
> _____
> _____
> _____
> _____

D A Y 5

WHISPERS OF UNBELIEF

I knew we would eventually get to this place, and honestly, I've been dreading it. I know I am supposed to be leading the charge here, but you must know my own hesitancy. *Beautiful.* It's an amazing word. It's an incredible pursuit. It's still hard to get my head around it sometimes.

When I began working on this Bible study, my friends said, "You're going to have to deal with the body-image stuff sooner rather than later. You can't wait until the end of the book. Our bodies are intertwined with every part of our identities and especially the longing for beautiful." I agree with their observations, but I still drag my heart.

Part of me wants to believe I am stronger than body image. That I can disconnect myself from the face in the mirror and live separately somehow. But I can't. It is all woven together. Our souls came inside these vessels we call bodies. The problem is that most of our lives we have looked at our bodies with earthly eyes and then let what we have seen assign value to our souls.

Every woman I know dreams of being the most beautiful woman in the room, with no prompting or prodding needed. She wants to be intellectual and witty, the one with great depth and insight, peaceful and spiritual. She dreams of being captivating. The heart of a woman longs for the completion and perfection we won't know until heaven. The heart longs to go home where it belongs, with God.

Until then, our body image keeps screaming that you can't become or captivate or improve until you lose 32 pounds, more or less. When you get the pounds off, there is a sag problem that needs the attention of a skilled surgeon. Oh yeah, those varicose veins are trouble. And that mid-life acne thing too. Actually, it seems as if there will always be something left to steal our peace in regard to body image. Anything and everything will be used to whisper into our ears, "Don't believe it, God couldn't really call you beautiful."

"Why am I so afraid that I don't measure up and never will?"

These next few days it won't do you any good to skip the questions that make you squirm. No one is looking. This is between you and God. Let the truth He reveals begin to set you free. Listen in your quiet prayer time for His voice of assurance and love. Still yourself and answer freely.

One day my counselor said, "Angela, I don't think you know very much about the love of God." He caught me off guard. I'm supposed to know a lot about that kind of stuff. Instead, I had listened to the whispers of unbelief and began to speak out of their deceit. I gave weight to the lies in my head.

I am praying that you and I will turn away from the whispers. That we will have eyes to see and tender hearts to respond to God's love for us. I am asking God to draw us even more deeply into the strength that comes from believing. I am asking Him to shout above the whispers, so that we can hear Him call us beautiful.

Before we begin, write a prayer below asking God to make things very clear to you in today's study. Ask Him to unmistakably highlight all the lies that whisper in your head and all the doubts that keep you from believing in His patient, pursuing, embracing love.

THE WHISPERS

Sometimes we hear the things we've said to ourselves. Sometimes it's the words of junior-high taunting. Sometimes it's the words we longed to hear but no one ever said.

I think if we'll put the whispers about body image on paper, some of their power will go away. We're going to put your body image on paper. I know, I'm reluctant too. Just go with me here.

Start with the good stuff and don't leave this part blank. Write at least five great traits about your physical appearance. Be specific. Remember the compliments you've received in the past.

_____

_____

_____

_____

_____

_____

Write out every frustration. Things you can never change, like the width of your ankles and things you would like to make different if you could. _____

_____

_____

_____

_____

_____

_____

If you want to come undone, just begin listening to the whispers of unbelief about God.

One of my friends said, "We live in a death culture. We speak death and darkness instead of life and goodness into one another's lives. God is a life giver." Could it be that the whispers you have heard about your body image have caused a part of your heart to die? Have they kept you from believing the life-giving truth that God wants you to hear? Journal your thoughts here.

_____

_____

_____

_____

_____

_____

_____

Knowing God purposefully created you just the way you are, what areas of your physical appearance or personality are you struggling to accept? _____

_____

_____

_____

_____

_____

Are you still struggling to believe God calls you beautiful? Ask the Lord to make it real to you in a way that lets you know it is Him. Ask Him to help you discover your beauty.

_____

_____

_____

_____

_____

_____

He has made everything beautiful in its time.

Ecclesiastes 3:11

Try to imagine the God-version of you. Imagine being the God who's in love with you and then tell me what He sees when He looks at you. What can you imagine He dreams for your life?

_____

_____

_____

_____

God has an artist's heart—He can look at a blank canvas and envision the masterpiece. Ask Him to tell you what He envisions for your future. What do you think the rest of your story might be from His perspective?

_____

_____

_____

_____

_____

_____

We've done a lot of heart work so far. Owning our God-given longings. Considering the people and things we love. Shedding light on the whispers about our beauty. I know some of this is heavy soul work, but press on my dear friend. God will give strength when you live in the truth of who you are. He will wrap up your tender heart and hold it close. Keep leaning into Him. Trust this process and watch to see how God is going to heal your wounds and set your heart free.

---

1. Brian Irwin, *Connected Hearts* (Longwood, FL: Xulon Press, 2002), 292-93.

2. H. Norman Wright, *Always Daddy's Girl* (Ventura, CA: Regal Books, 1989), 10.

3. Ibid., 193.

4. Ibid., 196-97.

The Shout

WEEK 3

The "shout" is the voice of God that comes and drowns out all the whispers of unbelief. The God of the universe has come in abounding love and compassion for such as us.

*When I consider your heavens,
    the work of your fingers,
the moon and the stars,
    which you have set in place,
what is man that you are mindful of him,*

the son of man that you care for him? (Psalm 8:3-4).

That God is mindful of me? That's huge. And grasping the whole thing is a gigantic step for most of us. The God of heaven knows us intimately.

Could it be that in His eyes we can find a reflection of ourselves that we have never known before? That in His reflection we are neither how we imagined ourselves to be nor thought of as we assumed? Could it be that God has been shouting His great love all the while, but we have buried our heads underneath the pillow of whispers, choosing to remain covered by the lies of this world and the deception of the Accuser?

Commit to listening for the voice of God this week. The times I have heard God speak into my heart, I have quieted myself in some way. Alone on the sofa. On my face on the floor in my closet. Outside on a hike. In a quieting posture or activity to let my soul settle so I can wait and listen.

Ask God to use these next days to speak like a shout into your soul.

VIEWER GUIDE

"So they brought him. When the spirit saw Jesus, it immediately threw the boy into a convulsion. He fell to the ground and rolled around, foaming at the mouth. Jesus asked the boy's father, 'How long has he been like this?' 'From childhood,' he answered. 'It has often thrown him into fire or water to kill him. But if you can do anything, take pity on us and help us.' "'If you can"?' said Jesus. 'Everything is possible for him who believes.' Immediately the boy's father exclaimed, 'I do believe; help me overcome my unbelief!'"
Mark 9:20-24

"Everything is possible for him who _____" (v. 23).

"I do _____; help me overcome my _____!" (v. 24).

Jesus says, "Just come on with your believing and your unbelief. I can work with that."

The clutter of the _____ can become familiar.

Do you know the difference between the Father's voice and the Accuser's voice?

The Father speaks truth:

     according to His _____

     according to His _____

     according to His _____ _____ _____

     according to His _____ _____ _____

When the Father calls a woman beautiful, then it's true.

CLINGING TO
THE WHISPERS

Memory Verse

He said to me, "My grace is sufficient for you, for my power is made perfect in weakness." Therefore I will boast all the more gladly about my weaknesses, so that Christ's power may rest on me.

2 Corinthians 12:9

We keep believing the same old things about ourselves and about God, simply out of habit. The messages from the media are so deeply entrenched in our culture that we have confused their voices with the voice of God. We mindlessly accept what the world calls beautiful and disregard the heart and passion of our Creator.

Why? Maybe we don't really know much about the love of God.

I'm going to ask some pointed questions about your relationship with God. I don't mean them to be accusations, but promptings to get us honest with ourselves. If the questions make you angry or make you squirm, could that be the Holy Spirit directing you toward change, greater understanding, or even repentance?

How would you rate your life with God right now?

❑close and intimate ❑surface and Sundays only

❑distant and rebellious ❑some other combination

Are you presently trusting God for anything powerful or waiting for Him to do the impossible? ❧ ❑ yes ❑ no ❧

If the answer is no, what in your life needs the powerful intervention of God? _____

_____

_____

_____

Have you seen God work in a powerful way in your life? ❧ ❑ yes ❑ no ❧ How? _____

_____

_____

Tell of a time you sensed the embracing love of God. A time when you knew He was present and holding you close.

_____

_____

_____

How do you respond when life doesn't turn out as you'd planned?

_____

_____

Do you run from your relationship with God, or do you lean into Him even when you feel disappointed or misunderstood?
❧ ❏ I run from God. ❏ I trust God. ❧

Do you live life with a sense of adventure, knowing you are held in the arms of God, or do you live hesitantly, believing one wrong move could ruin everything? ❧ ❏ I'm always up for an adventure! ❏ You can never be too careful. ❧

Do you look more like Jesus this year than you did last year? Are you growing up spiritually? Are you becoming more and more like Him, less and less like you? ❧ ❏ yes ❏ no ❧ ❏ I think I'm about the same. ❧

Sometimes we get stuck and stop growing for a season. Life keeps us spinning for a hundred different reasons. And in the spin, our spiritual lives can fall fast asleep. You can show up at church, sit right in the presence of God, but never really get it because your soul is snoring. I don't want to beat you up. I want to lavish you with grace, but if the Holy Spirit is trying to wake up your sleepy soul, then roll over and get out of bed!

We never become women of great faith without the continued pursuit of maturity. Lack of spiritual maturity will keep you clinging to the whispers.

LEARNING HOW TO BELIEVE

Learn how to believe that God calls you beautiful. Don't let it overwhelm you. This one is going to take time, but what an amazing gift it will be to your soul. One of the first steps in learning how to believe is learning what the voice of God sounds like.

Sometimes I have to stop and ask myself, "Am I hearing the voice of God or the voice of the Accuser?" The Accuser is our enemy, Satan. Anytime God begins doing a work in our lives, Satan begins a parallel work to try and distract us. When God wants to speak to us, Satan wants to interrupt so we can't hear. He might feed us a lie or offer us an imitation to get us off track.

If you believe a lie, it affects you. Satan will do everything he can to get you to believe the whispers. He has observed your life and knows your weak places, the buttons that get you distracted and the issues that paralyze your soul. He likes to talk about all that stuff because it keeps you from believing and living in the truths of God.

You shaped me first
  inside, then out;
  you formed me in
  my mother's womb.
I thank you, High God—
  you're breathtaking!
  Body and soul, I am
  marvelously made!
  I worship in adoration—
  what a creation!
You know me inside
  and out,
  you know every bone
  in my body;
You know exactly how
  I was made, bit by bit,
  how I was sculpted
  from nothing into
  something.
  Like an open book,
  you watched me
  grow from
  conception to birth;
all the stages of my life
  were spread out
  before you,
The days of my life all
  prepared
before I'd even lived
  one day.

Psalm 139:13-16, THE MESSAGE

53

We all need a regular exchange in our souls. We must replace the lies of Satan with the truth of God. We can't just psych ourselves into believing. We can't grit our teeth and force ourselves to believe. The process of exchange takes time. We go forward, slide back, and then have to regain lost ground.

"Some people are like seed along the path, where the word is sown. As soon as they hear it, Satan comes and takes away the word that was sown in them."

Mark 4:15

When I tell you God calls you beautiful, what thoughts immediately pop into your head? _____

_____

_____

_____

_____

Are those thoughts more nearly the voice of God speaking truth into your life or the voice of the Accuser who wants to keep wounding you? ❧ ❏ God   ❏ the Accuser ❧

The Accuser uses a false imitation of the Holy Spirit's convicting power. Satan always spotlights sin, even sin when it has been forgiven and covered by the grace of God. Satan does it to discourage and depress. He will keep reminding you of your sin as long as you listen (Revelation 12:10).

The Accuser tries to bring confusion to us by planting weeds among good seed. The good that God has sown in our lives, Satan tries to choke out with weeds (Matthew 13:38-39).

The Accuser wants to squelch the truth in our lives with lies until we are rendered completely useless (1 Peter 5:8).

"[Satan] was a murderer from the beginning, not holding to the truth, for there is no truth in him. When he lies, he speaks his native language, for he is a liar and the father of lies."

John 8:44

Satan	God
spotlights sin and keeps reminding you.	forgives repented-of sin and remembers it no more.
tries to make you confused.	wants to make your path clear.
keeps you wounded with repetitive lies.	heals wounds and replaces lies with truth.
reminds you what the world says.	tells you what He has said.
disappoints you with cheap imitations.	rewards you with real gifts and blessings.
never stops trying another way to trip you up.	never stops providing abundant strength for resistance.

You may need others to help you distinguish between the voice of the Accuser and the voice of God. Sometimes it can feel presumptuous to embrace what God is saying about *you* as truth.

You may need people to go the journey with you. People who can help you discover what God is saying, confirm His voice, discern the words of the Accuser, and stop inclining your head toward the whispers.

Satan's lies will only be silenced by listening to God's voice.

What kind of person should you align yourself with for a spiritual journey of learning and depth? Read the description below and underline the important characteristics.

> She is a woman of known integrity and safety. She must be the keeper of your heart. A woman who has known brokenness and healing. Someone who is running fast and strong toward God in spiritual things. She is a little further down the road than you. A woman who is alive with passion and desires adventure. A woman who lives and gives the grace and mercy of Jesus. This one is a rare bird. Make her dinner. Clean her oven. Do anything to get next to her.
>
> Someone who is growing and becoming open to the work of God, even outside her theological box. Run from legalists and those who seem to have all the answers tied up with a bow.

Do you know a woman who can come alongside you in the journey? ☐ yes ☐ I can't think of anyone. If yes, who is she?

_____

If no, pray that God will bring to your mind a friend who can accompany you. Even if she is far away, pursue an honest relationship with her.

_____
_____
_____
_____
_____
_____
_____
_____
_____
_____
_____
_____

DAY 2

HELP MY UNBELIEF

Some would have us think we can say something positive about ourselves over and over until we believe it. We could chant, "I am beautiful; I am beautiful," in some quiet meditation until it is so.

We've heard our souls long for beautiful, but believing what God says of us is the hinge on which this whole journey turns. If we don't believe God, then how do we go on from here? Do we just default and live vicariously? Do we watch the beautiful people and track their lives of adventure? Do we relegate ourselves to observation in place of becoming?

If you choose not to believe God on this one, what will the results in your life look like?

_____

_____

What are you choosing for yourself emotionally, mentally, and spiritually when you decide not to believe God calls you beautiful?

_____

_____

If you truly believe God calls you beautiful, how does that color how you live and make choices?

_____

_____

I love the story in Mark 9:17-24. How do you come to God in belief? Do you keep trying to help Him along toward the answers you want? Or have you learned to rest in your belief, trusting that whatever you ask of God, He's on it? He doesn't forget? He doesn't get distracted?

Coming to believe that God calls you beautiful means overcoming your unbelief. You can resist believing for a million reasons. Maybe you hesitate because with believing comes responsibility. If you believe God, things might change. You would have to change your perspective—how you perceive the world and your purpose.

"Everything is possible for him who believes." Immediately the boy's father exclaimed, "I do believe; help me overcome my unbelief!"

Mark 9:23-24

What might begin to change in your life if you rest in the truth of being known as beautiful?_____

_____

_____

What responsibility would come to you in believing that?

_____

_____

_____

Maybe you thought that believing means you are finally calm and peaceful on the inside. That you are without hesitancy. Read John 11:38-44 in the margin.

What did Martha say to Jesus when He got to the tomb of Lazarus and asked for the stone to be rolled away? _____

_____

I smile at Martha because she is so me. She is anxious and says, "But, Lord," offering her own wise observation. When you hear that God calls you beautiful, have you been saying, "But, Lord"?

How does Jesus respond to Martha? _____

_____

After the stone was removed, Jesus called Lazarus back from the dead. Jesus was not frustrated by the anxious "But, Lord" of Martha. Then Martha obeyed and took away the stone, even in her anxiety, so she could see the glory of God.

God is not frustrated by your "But, Lord" either. Voice your anxiety and believe anyway. This is the avenue by which we get to see the glory of God.

Believing does not always arise out of peace and calm. The father of the possessed son in Mark 9 was hesitant and weak, and yet he leaned into a trust beyond what he could imagine. Believing is choosing obedience and responding out of trust, even when we cannot see.

How is God calling you to obedience with these truths? Specifically, what steps of obedience can you take to believe that God calls you beautiful, in spite of the anxiety and the "But, Lord"?

_____

_____

Write a prayer confessing your own doubts and unbelief. God is not put off by your struggles. He does not wag a finger in disdain at your honesty. _____

_____ _____

_____

_____

_____

Jesus, once more deeply moved, came to the tomb. It was a cave with a stone laid across the entrance. "Take away the stone," he said. "But, Lord," said Martha, the sister of the dead man, "by this time there is a bad odor, for he has been there four days." Then Jesus said, "Did I not tell you that if you believed, you would see the glory of God?" So they took away the stone. Then Jesus looked up and said, "Father, I thank you that you have heard me. I knew that you always hear me, but I said this for the benefit of the people standing here, that they may believe that you sent me." When he had said this, Jesus called in a loud voice, "Lazarus, come out!" The dead man came out, his hands and feet wrapped with strips of linen, and a cloth around his face. Jesus said to them, "Take off the grave clothes and let him go."

John 11:38-44

We were created with the need to be affirmed. I imagine that from cradle until grave we will always long for validation, to know that someone sees our accomplishments, and as women, to know that someone calls us beautiful.

Today, let's celebrate God. He gives soul affirmation and deep, soul filling. Hallelujah.

D A Y   3

NOISE AND CLUTTER

The past few months I have been plagued by noise and clutter. It is so incredibly distracting. I want to dance. I hear the music in the background, but I can't enter in because the stuff in my head makes me dizzy. The noise seems louder and bigger than the invitation from God to dance in His arms.

I can deal with what noise and clutter I find and move along, only to learn a little later that new noise and clutter has come a-callin'. Removing the noise and clutter from my life is an ongoing process. Maybe it's the same for you.

As long as we are breathing and moving about, interacting with people and family, words will come to us and make us their hostages. Situations will interrupt our plans and sidetrack our travels. Days will come when we will move without feeling. Sometimes life seems so heavy. We can quickly begin to feel numb. God seems far away when our heads are filled with noise and clutter.

I can work along for months, loving and living creatively, spontaneously, and deliberately. Then noise will collect in my head, clutter will trip up my heart, and suddenly I'm stuck. I can wake up emotionally and spiritually paralyzed, unable to sort out the overwhelming distractions. I guess you're not much different from me; we can all become distracted and stuck.

My prayer for you is that these next days will prompt you to acknowledge the noise in your head and the clutter in your life. And then I am asking God to make you willing to do whatever it takes to remove everything that stands between you and His embrace.

TURN IT DOWN IN THERE

In the last few days, we have talked about the whispers of unbelief, those murmurs we hear in our heads about what God thinks of us. The murmurs that tell us not to believe God.

The noise that keeps me from the dance sounds something like this:

Have I missed something? You mean this is all there is to life?
I've wasted so much time.
What was I made for?
It's all my fault.
Who have I become, and who is the real me?
My life doesn't count for much. I'm not sure it's all worth it.
My sin is too big.
My scars are too painful.
I'm an embarrassment.
I will never be beautiful.
Somebody get me out of here.
Time is running out. Hurry up and do something.

Begin thinking and taking inventory. How does the noise in your head manifest itself? What do your doubts say? _____

_____

_____

_____

_____

_____

_____

What questions or thoughts haunt your days?

_____

_____

_____

_____

This kind of noise can be like a thread woven through everything you do. How does the noise in your head paralyze your life or keep you from living in power? _____

_____

_____

_____

_____

Sometimes we can let the noise in our heads become our false identity. We have listened to it so long that we have come to believe the noise represents all there is of us. Sometimes women will hear labels such as *old maid, divorced, loser, slow learner, driven,* or *broken.* The labels attach themselves to our noise, and we let them define us.

What are some names you either call yourself or others have called you that have become your false identity?

_____

_____

_____

What does God call you? _____

_____

_____

_____

Remember the voice of the Accuser? Weed him out of this discussion. Listen for God through the Holy Spirit.

> The Holy Spirit will bring conviction.
> The Accuser wants to bring shame.
> The Holy Spirit speaks to us about freedom and release from sin.
> The Accuser wants to keep us in bondage.
> The Holy Spirit convicts us clearly and specifically about an action, attitude, or misguided belief.
> The Accuser promotes confusion and blame.
> The Holy Spirit prompts us toward confession and repentance so we can hear God's heart of love.
> The Accuser wants us to believe that we are eternally condemned.
> God might say, "You didn't tell the truth."
> The Accuser would say, "You are a liar."
> The Holy Spirit wants to clear out the noise that distracts you from dancing with God.
> The Accuser wants to leave you in a heap in the shadows.

There may be other effective ways to deal with the voices and their accusations, but I know of only one: powerful and passionate prayer. I recommend prayer as the tool for quieting your soul.

AN EXERCISE IN PRAYER

You may begin alone, but asking someone to pray with you can be helpful. A counselor may be helpful if the noise in your head is particularly painful. A close friend may feel safer for you. Ask God to direct.

This isn't a one-time deal, but instead a push to get you in. Kind of like diving into the deep end of the pool instead of slowly working your way down the steps. The idea is to learn to swim and become a strong swimmer; I'm asking you to jump in and get wet in prayer.

Are you afraid to pray out loud so that someone else can hear and respond to you in prayer? Try praying aloud when you are alone in the car or at home in your room. It will get you accustomed to the sound of your voice in prayer. No need to talk differently or whisper; just speak what comes to mind. Begin learning what it "feels" like to speak your prayers.

Refer back to your list of noises on page 59 and choose one of the questions or thoughts that haunt your days. As you begin to pray through it, you may realize there is other pain or emotion attached. Take notes if you need to.

Ask God about the particular thought you have chosen. Ask Him where that idea came from. Who gave it to you?

_____

_____

_____

_____

Ask Him to tell you if it is true. What is He saying to you?

_____

_____

_____

_____

Ask God very specifically what He says of this idea in your head.

_____

_____

_____

_____

What does He want you to do with it? Where does He want you to go with it? To whom would He like for you to speak, if necessary?

_____

_____

_____

Ask God for continued insight into the particular noise. Tell Him He can wake you up in the middle of the night if He needs you—whatever it takes to understand the noise and quiet the voices.

This kind of intense praying is not without emotion. It may be draining for you in many ways, and sometimes you have to wait until you are ready to pray, listen, and receive. On the other hand, you can't keep procrastinating or you'll never deal with the noise. That's the reason we're here.

Our goal is to tear down cracked foundations and rebuild in strength, yet run from being self-absorbed or obsessed. I want you to know who you are in God, but to get there we have to weed through all the junk in your head that has given you a false identity. I want you to be able to clearly ask, "Who does God say that I am?" and believe it.

PUTTING YOUR STUFF AWAY

Today we're on to soul clutter. Do you know clutter? It's the stuff I put on the stairs in my house so I'll remember to take it up the next time I go. Then I walk right past it. I mean to pick it up, but somehow I don't. Eventually, I run past even more junk, and before I know it I have clutter—a lot of it. And what's worse is I can get used to it. I know a stack of towels, two puzzles, and a bottle of shampoo don't belong on the stairs, but I can still run past them all day long.

In just the same way, clutter comes to our souls. It's the stuff we've climbed over and ignored, thinking we'll get around to it eventually. Soul clutter is the collection of emotional, relational, and spiritual issues we have been stepping over. Each one needs to be picked up, sorted, and put away. Clutter can keep us tripping and stumbling for a lifetime.

Here's a list of issues to get you thinking. Review the entire list but choose three to five to write about. As you consider them, ask yourself: *Have these things stood between me and God? What needs my attention?* Make personal notes as you go. Feel free to add others that aren't on my list. Respond to each issue honestly.

overscheduling	gossip
isolation	lying
rebellion	rejection
drivenness and perfectionism	fears
envy	legalism
insecurity	depression
anger	bitterness
obsessions	body image
relationships	sabotaging your health
addictions	unforgiveness

Issue: _____
Its role in your life: _____
_____
_____
_____
_____

Issue: _____
Its role in your life: _____
_____
_____
_____
_____

Issue: _____
Its role in your life: _____
_____
_____
_____
_____

Issue: _____
Its role in your life: _____
_____
_____
_____
_____

Issue: _____
Its role in your life: _____
_____
_____
_____
_____

I imagine some of the clutter in your soul is beginning to surface. Now what? Let's begin with baby steps.

Acknowledge the mess. It may require getting messy to get clean, and it could take a while to get things sorted out. Acknowledge your mess in prayer. It's OK to lay this big pile of clutter before the Lord and ask Him where to begin. I can't think of a better place to turn with your heavy load.

Realize you may have to call for help. You and I belong to the body of Christ, and Scripture instructs us to carry one another's burdens. Sometimes you can crumble underneath the weight. You don't have to go through this alone to prove you are superhuman or super-spiritual.

Think of three people in your life who might be safe, available, and mature enough to walk with you. You may only need one, but think of three. List their names here.

_____

_____

_____

Pray and seek prayer covering. Nothing powerful happens in your life apart from prayer. To begin to deal with the clutter in your soul will require power that overcomes weakness. Begin on your knees. Ask others to cover you in prayer. They don't have to know everything. They can pray for strength and wisdom.

Expect this season of reconciling, reordering, and repairing to take longer than you think it will. Life should come with a warning label: "Everything takes longer than you expect." That principle is especially true with soul work. To recognize the clutter in your life is only the beginning. To sort it all out and put it away can take a while.

Begin now. To delay any longer is to allow more clutter to crowd your way.

Journal. Some of you do and some of you don't. Would you give it a try? Draw pictures if you have to. Doodles and diagrams of the steps you are taking. The dreams you are dreaming. Some women love to scrapbook. Consider journaling the scrapbook of your soul.

Allow God to lavish you with His grace. I have met very few people who know much about the grace of God. I am a devoted student, only beginning to learn of His incredible riches of grace. I love 2 Corinthians 12:9: "My grace is sufficient for you."

> *The other evening I was riding home after a heavy day's work. I felt wearied, and sore depressed, when swiftly and suddenly that text came to me, "My grace is sufficient for [you]." I reached home and looked it up in the original, and at last it came to me in this way. "My grace is sufficient for THEE." And I said, "I should think it is, Lord," and I burst out laughing … It seemed to make unbelief so absurd. O brethren, be great believers. Little faith will bring your souls to heaven, but great faith will bring heaven to your souls.*
>
> —*C. H. Spurgeon* [1]

Allow God to lavish you with His grace. Don't keep beating yourself up. Most of us are prone to guilt. So much guilt in fact that we become paralyzed by the process and choke out the good work God is doing. Let God forgive, heal, restore, soothe, mend, and strengthen. That is grace, and God has plenty of it for you and for me. You cannot drink dry the river of grace or breathe the last of God's gifts for you.

You cannot drink dry the river of grace or breathe the last of God's gifts for you.

THE EYE OF THE BEHOLDER

All that truly matters is the eye of the beholder, and God is the supreme Beholder. So why have we listened to the noise in our heads for so long? Why have we tripped over the same clutter for years? Make up your mind to be free of these distractions so you can hear what the Beholder has to say about you.

It has been a scary prayer to pray, but I have learned that God comes when I say, "OK, God, whatever it takes, I'm ready. I want to get to work on my soul. Come and work in power for Your glory." And He always comes in mercy. Expect Him to be gentle and loving. Expect Him to begin healing. Expect His great joy over your new heart and desire to change.

What is the Beholder saying to you today? Sit still and listen. Write what you hear with your heart.

_____

_____

_____

_____

_____

_____

_____

_____

_____

_____

_____

_____

_____

_____

_____

_____

_____

_____

_____

DAY 5

SOMETIMES THE PRODIGAL, SOMETIMES THE ELDER BROTHER

I love the story Jesus tells about the prodigal son and the elder brother. I'm drawn to this story because I know the ending and I love what happens. At the end, the God of Heaven runs to hold us. I'm not over it. I hope I never get over the truth of mercy and grace. I hope I never grow hardened to the pursuing love of God. I hope you don't either.

> Read Luke 15:11-32 in your Bible and soak in each word of Jesus' parable.

Close your eyes and picture the Father running to you. Not when you've gotten it all figured out and 'fessed up, but right now, in the midst of your life. Today— in your kitchen, at your desk, or sitting on top of your bed. Wherever you are, imagine the God of the universe running to hold you.

I am sitting on my sofa with a laptop on my knees. I have on jeans and an old Carolina sweatshirt. No makeup and day-old hair. Books are scattered everywhere, and the dryer is running. The house is quiet because the kids are at school, but there are little reminders of them everywhere.

> Stop where you are and picture God. I am closing my eyes to imagine with you. Don't go any further until you really stop and close your eyes. I don't want you to miss this one.
>
> What picture do you have in your head?
>
> _____
>
> _____
>
> What does God whisper as you fall into His arms?
>
> _____
>
> _____
>
> _____
>
> _____
>
> _____

I imagined the Lord scooping me into His arms and resting my head on His shoulder. Right then is when the tears came. I think they are tears of relief. They feel like little-girl tears in a woman's body. God must know how desperately a woman longs to be held. I forget until a moment like this. I cry because I don't have to be the strongest one anymore. I cry because it feels as if He whispers, "It's OK, Angela. You don't have to worry so much. I'll take it from here."

I HAVE BEEN A PRODIGAL

This parable is so powerful, let's watch it unfold. Reread verses 11-13.

Maybe you've never thought of yourself as a prodigal. Or maybe you've known the truth all along. Anytime you or I willfully choose to turn away from God even though we know better, we are prodigals.

Sometimes we think of prodigals only as sons or daughters who have run away from home and chosen wild living. Those are definitely prodigals, but there is more to being a prodigal than just being a rebellious child. I believe a prodigal is someone who has squandered the wealth God has given—those of us who know better and still choose poorly, willfully choosing the distraction over the dance with God.

> "There was a man who had two sons. The younger one said to his father, 'Father, give me my share of the estate.' So he divided his property between them. Not long after that, the younger son got together all he had, set off for a distant country and there squandered his wealth in wild living."
>
> Luke 15:11-13

Think about the wealth you have been given because of God. What is your share of His estate? _____

_____

_____

What gifts has the Father given to you?

_____

_____

_____

_____

_____

When we turn away from God, we leave the dance and wander into the distant country. Have you ever taken everything God has given to you and just left?   ❏ yes   ❏ no

Where would you place yourself right now?
❏ at the dance, in the arms of God
❏ at the dance, standing in the shadows
❏ thinking about taking my inheritance and getting out of here
❏ driving off to the distant country
❏ living in the faraway land for quite some time

LIFE IN THE FARAWAY LAND

"After he had spent everything, there was a severe famine in that whole country, and he began to be in need. So he went and hired himself out to a citizen of that country, who sent him to his fields to feed pigs. He longed to fill his stomach with the pods that the pigs were eating, but no one gave him anything."

Luke 15:14-16

Continue reading with Luke 15:14-16.

We have heard it said many times that sin takes you further than you ever intended to go, costs you more than you ever intended to pay, and keeps you longer than you ever intended to stay. It's the story of the prodigal.

When our supply of grace runs out, God gives more. When we lack forgiveness, it is ours for the asking. When we are in need of wisdom, God provides. His good gifts to us are always being replenished because He is pouring Himself into our emptiness. We are partakers of His wealth because we are daughters of the Father.

When we pack up what we have been given and drive off in search of something better, the riches come to an end. We will spend everything we brought and begin to be in need. Like the prodigal, we can find ourselves empty and broke, feeding pigs in a sty.

If you've ever found yourself in a faraway land, turning from God, describe where you ended up. _____

_____

_____

_____

Describe what called (or continues to call) you away from the dance with God. Addictions? Obsessions? Curiosity?

_____

_____

_____

Understanding what tempts you to leave the arms of God could be a huge step toward change. Knowing where you might be tripped can help you be prepared the next time. Are you willing to ask a close friend what she sees? I've given a couple of people I respect permission to say the hard things. I hate it, but the work it does in my soul is worth it. If you can't let someone in, at least be honest with yourself about temptation.

In what ways do you or your friend see you turning from God?

_____

_____

_____

_____

Maybe you have wandered away like the prodigal sometime in your past. Maybe you are far away from God right now. Maybe you feel the allure of the distant country and are considering a trip there soon. Wherever you are, read what Jesus says in Luke 15:17-20.

My favorite phrase in that passage is, "When he came to his senses" (v. 17). Do you see the application for our own lives? Whatever has distracted us. Wherever it has taken us. No matter how long we've been away. You and I can come to our senses.

Do you remember a time of "coming to your senses"? Describe it.

_____

_____

_____

Eugene Peterson, author of *The Message,* implies in his paraphrase of this passage that the lowliness of the pigsty brought the prodigal to his senses. How far will you have to go until you "come to your senses"?

Coming to your senses might mean:
• turning from repetitive, plaguing sin or foolish living.
• turning or running from an unhealthy relationship.
• becoming awake to the life and possibilities ahead of you. Dreaming again.
• beginning new habits that improve your life.
• refocusing on your family.
• making a new commitment to spiritual passion.
• seeking counseling or professional help for emotional wounds.
• regaining or forging a sense of order and purpose for living.

What would it look like in your life to "come to your senses" right now, no more delays? Write out a prayer of returning. _____

_____

_____

_____

_____

_____

No matter what you have written or realized or prayed about today, keep the ending in mind. God runs.

> When he came to his senses, he said, "How many of my father's hired men have food to spare, and here I am starving to death! I will set out and go back to my father and say to him: Father, I have sinned against heaven and against you. I am no longer worthy to be called your son; make me like one of your hired men." So he got up and went to his father. But while he was still a long way off, his father saw him and was filled with compassion for him; he ran to his son, threw his arms around him and kissed him.
>
> Luke 15:17-20

---

1. William Williams, *Personal Remembrances of Charles Haddon Spurgeon* (London: Passmore and Alabaster, 1895), 231, quoted in Larry J. Michael, *Spurgeon on Leadership* (Grand Rapids: Kregel, 2003), 186-87.

A Pursuing Heart

WEEK 4

Inside the tight embrace of God your life will finally be free. Can you hear Him saying to you, "In My arms you will be free"?

Whether you are the prodigal who has wandered away from the dance or the elder brother who can't hear the music, it's a miserable place to be. Both keep us separate from God and the dance He has for our lives.

Over and over again, the same will be true. When there are distractions. When the world tries to cut in. When we trip over our two left feet and feel frustrated. The answer is always and only *Jesus*. The answer will always be *return to the arms of God*.

Is there a returning that still needs to happen in your life? Have you been dragging your heart?

I want you to know the freedom Christ can bring to your life. I want you to live the message of Galatians 5:1: "It is for freedom that Christ has set us free."

I want you to hear God call you beautiful. I want you to rejoice in His lavish gifts and enduring love. I want you to dance!

VIEWER GUIDE

We all have _____ - _____ woman potential.

Characteristics of a weak-willed woman:

The weak-willed woman has a _____!

The bullies of fear run away when the hero called _____ _____ comes to the rescue.

When God holds back the punishment we deserve, we call that _____.

When He does it over and over again, we call that _____.

PRODIGALS LIKE YOU AND ME

Memory Verse

Flee the evil desires
of youth, and pursue
righteousness, faith, love
and peace, along with
those who call on the
Lord out of a pure heart.

2 Timothy 2:22

You are probably not a typical prodigal. You're probably not like my friend Rob who kept being called away into his life of drug and alcohol addiction. One jail cell to another. One rehab, then the next. But when you consider the prodigal idea for yourself, the whole point is to ask yourself honestly:

Is there any hidden sin that distracts me from God?
❏ yes ❏ no

What is that sin?

_____

_____

Where does that sin take me in secret?

_____

_____

Do you live separate lives? One in front of your family and one in secret? You can actually live a secret life or you can be planning one in your head. Both are incredibly dangerous.

Every God-begotten
person conquers the
world's ways. The
conquering power that
brings the world to its
knees is our faith. The
person who wins out over
the world's ways is simply
the one who believes
Jesus is the Son of God.

1 JOHN 5:4–5, THE MESSAGE

If you live or plan separate lives, what are they?

_____

_____

_____

What does your heart long for that the secret life seems to offer?

_____

_____

What if someone could pull up the history on your computer, collect the receipts from your credit cards, or see everything you've watched on television? What would they find? Would you be OK with that? What behavior or pattern do you want to keep hidden?

_____

_____

_____

Do you hear the voice of God calling you back to the dance and refuse to answer? ❧ ❑ yes ❑ no ❧ If so, what holds you back?

_____

_____

_____

_____

_____

Your ordinary, run-of-the-mill prodigal can be a woman like you or me. She is a woman whose heart is becoming harder. She is squandering her life and all the riches God has given her. She probably knows she is not dancing but has decided at some level that she doesn't care anymore. She may be living openly or secretly. Either way, an ever-growing distance is growing between her and the Father.

The prodigal will always, ultimately, find herself longing to go home.

Eventually the allure runs out. The distant country and its emptiness begin to stink like a pigsty. The prodigal will always, ultimately, find herself longing to go home.

WATCHING FOR OUR RETURN

Read Luke 15:20 in the margin. You might want to underline this one in your Bible.

> Imagine God running to you, embracing you, and kissing you. What is your response to the picture of God running to you? Do you want to run toward Him or run away from His embrace?

_____

_____

_____

When he was still a long way off, his father saw him. His heart pounding, he ran out, embraced him, and kissed him.

Luke 15:20, THE MESSAGE

Sometimes we believe we can only allow ourselves to be embraced by God when we have decided we are pure enough or repentant enough. Nothing in this parable tells us the son came home with pure motives and a pure heart. He came home intending to live as a servant to get away from the pigsty and pig food. He came home because he had nowhere else to go.

Maybe you get to the place of understanding that God calls you beautiful and even enter into His embrace. But then the whispers start: *You'll never stay pure enough. You can't hold it all together. You're going to lose the embrace of God.*

Even if we don't understand a holy God running toward a self-centered, manipulative, sinful woman, it is still true. God still runs. I hear you protesting, "But you don't know me." I don't have to. I know the Father heart of God, and He will run to hold you.

GOING HOME

Read Luke 15:21-24. How many times have you stayed locked down in the prison of *no longer worthy* (v. 21)? I have a friend whose father told her when she was growing up, "You are a stupid idiot, and you'll never be worth anything." If her dad weren't dead, I'd want to hit him. Can you imagine what that does to the soul? She heard it all her life. Now he's gone, and it's still all she can hear. Most of us didn't hear those words growing up but remain stuck in the land of *no longer worthy*.

Here's the deal, and I hope it comes as a huge relief for you: we were not worthy, even when we thought maybe we were. Becoming worthy of the Father doesn't have anything to do with our performance. We can't get good enough. Look cute enough. Act pure enough. We become made worthy of the Father's love because we ask Jesus to cover us with His forgiveness. Jesus makes us lovely to the Father. Jesus covers our sin. Through Jesus, we belong to God.

If you still feel *no longer worthy*, ask yourself these questions:

> Do I feel guilty?
> Have I been unable to clean my slate?
> Do I feel I've offended God?
> Have I abused others?
> Do I carry anger and judgment?
> Do I harbor unforgiveness?
> Have I looked to counterfeit sources for intimacy?
> Do I feel shame?
> Have I been abused?
> > Disgraced?
> > Dishonored?
> > Humiliated?
> > Exposed?
> > Accused?
> > Spit on?

Because of guilt and shame, we can decide that we are not worthy of the Father's arms and run away in our embarrassment.

How is the Holy Spirit prompting you to deal with these ideas about worth, guilt, and shame?

_____

_____

_____

_____

The world assigns value to a woman for many reasons—her aptitude, her skills, her body, or her overall life performance. When the Father runs to hold you, when He invites you to dance the dance of your life in His arms, it is not about your performance. It's about your identity. He runs to you because you belong to Him. And you belong to Him because you have believed in Jesus as His Son. That's it. End of discussion. When you belong to Jesus, you are worthy to the Father.

You can protest. Lament your sin. Wallow in your choices. Choose to continue in unbelief. Doesn't matter what you do—that's not the point. The point is, the blood of Jesus covers your heart and makes you beautiful to the Father.

The blood of Jesus covers your heart and makes you beautiful to the Father.

Now that, my sister, is something to throw a party about. It's what the Father did, and it's good reason for you to celebrate His goodness for the rest of your life.

Would you say your life is woven with threads of celebration?
❏ yes ❏ no

What and how do you celebrate?

_____
_____
_____
_____

Are you on the lookout for the smallest victories that need a celebration or party? ❏ yes ❏ no

Look around your life and your family. Who needs a victory party?
For what?_____
_____
_____
_____
_____

Plan something in the next few weeks. What about a batch of cookies (baked or bought) or some flowers (grown or purchased) that would celebrate a friendship? Life is much too short. Dance the happy dance with someone today.

Life is much too short. Dance the happy dance with someone today.

Are you making a big deal about the goodness of God? Don't you think it's time? What about a gathering of people you love just to celebrate the blessings of God? After a bowl of ice cream shared with friends who talk about the great gifts of God, no one will leave lonely or miserable or discouraged.

What can you commit to today to celebrate God?

I HAVE BEEN THE ELDER BROTHER

Today we're going to talk about the "good one," the one who stayed home. Sometimes we have been the prodigal. But sometimes we can be the elder brother.

Read Luke 15:25-32. This may not apply to you. I kind of wish it didn't apply so completely to me. We elder brother types are fairly gross.

I talked to an elder brother woman on the phone the other day. I had not heard someone be so blatantly the elder brother in a while. I heard legalism. I heard haughtiness that made me shudder. I heard judgment. I heard a woman in ministry being the snotty elder brother. I remembered my own years there, and I ached. My words to her fell on deaf ears. I just wanted to get off the phone. Elder brothers are self-righteous, and you can't really tell them anything. One day they just get whacked over the head with their own piety. Maybe that's how they come to their senses.

If you feel there is an outside shot that your life falls under the heading of elder brother, please don't wait until you get whacked. If you hear God speaking to you in these pages, don't harden your heart. Allow yourself to be tender and receive direction from the Holy Spirit. You don't want to live any longer in haughtiness. It's a prison everyone else can see, but you don't even know you're in it.

With that in mind, let's work through some of these thoughts about the elder brother.

The prodigal knew he was a sinner. The elder brother could not see his own sinfulness.

Do you have eyes to see inside your own heart, or can you just see what's wrong with everyone else? ❧ ❑ I can see my own sin. ❑ I only see the sins of others. ❧

What elder brother traits can you see in your own heart?

_____

_____

_____

_____

Are you "religious" for the sake of appearance? ❧ ❑ yes ❑ no ❧

Does keeping the "rules" make you feel safe? ❧ ❑ yes ❑ no ❧

What religious rules make you feel safe?

_____

_____

_____

How do you respond when someone blows it and breaks a rule?

_____

_____

_____

Do you offer a heart of compassion or a heart of judgment?
❑ compassion ❑ judgment

If judgment, what sends you immediately to that response instead
of grace?_____

_____

_____

Are you afraid of extending grace? ❑ yes ❑ no Why would
that be true?_____

_____

_____

_____

_____

*The elder brother thought the father loved him because he was hardworking
and faithful.*

Have you believed that obedience earns you the Father's love?
❑ yes ❑ no

Write what you know about receiving the Father's love. How does it
come to us, and why?_____

_____

_____

_____

Do you understand that obedience is our gift back to God for His
love? ❑ yes ❑ no

How does your life reflect your gift of obedience?

_____

_____

How do you desire to give more in this area?

_____

_____

_____

Because the elder brother had not known grace, he was not able to extend grace. Do you know a woman who knows about living and giving grace? Do whatever you can to get close to her. I can write to you about it, but I'm not sure you can get "living in grace" until you bump up against someone who has it and it rubs off on you.

You cannot give what you do not have. Pray about this. Ask God for more.

Write a prayer for a friend and giver of grace.

_____

_____

_____

_____

_____

The elder brother was bound by unforgiveness. When you come to understand how much you have already been forgiven by the Father, you want to give that to someone else. The elder-brother-type woman doesn't get it. She holds on to unforgiveness, and it keeps her locked in a cage from the inside out. She has the key for escape—to begin forgiving.

Do you have a list? What if you just began forgiving everyone you could think of for no good reason except that you have been forgiven in Jesus? What if they don't deserve it and you forgive them anyway? How do you think it would feel to be released from grudge bondage? It would feel wonderful. So wonderful, you might get to dancing. Write about it. Pray about it. Journal about it. But don't stop there. Forgive every one of them and be free.

The elder brother didn't know he had always possessed the riches of the father. The riches of the father belonged to both the prodigal and to his brother. We are also partakers because we belong to God.

Have you said thank you lately? Remember God's blessings and lavish gifts. Write out a prayer of praise to Him.

_____

_____

_____

_____

_____

_____

The elder brother didn't hear the music with his heart. He didn't know he'd been invited to the dance.

Are you missing the music and the celebration of life?
❏ yes ❏ no

If so, what happened? _____
_____
_____

Does anything make you laugh anymore? ❏ yes ❏ no

How can you begin to return to laughter and a joyful heart?
_____
_____
_____

THE WAY OF THE ELDER BROTHER

Have you been the elder brother? ❏ yes ❏ no

Do you find yourself struggling with his demeanor?
❏ yes ❏ no

How and why? _____
_____
_____

Underneath the self-righteousness is usually a woman fueled by fear, pain, and sorrow. Circle the fears that belong to you. Use the lines below to elaborate on these fears or add other fears that aren't listed.

rejection   betrayal   exposure
abandonment   insecurities   consequences of sin

_____
_____
_____
_____
_____
_____

We'll talk more about our fears later. Until then, make notes on the ideas that seem to press into your heart. If you realize that underneath your attitude is a spirit of fear, then begin taking it to God in prayer.

The issues listed below can fuel the same elder-brother attitude.
Again, circle any of the items that apply and elaborate as you feel led.

loss and disappointment
making sacrifices
mental anguish
divorce or broken relationships

suffering
physical affliction
allowing bitterness to grow
loneliness

_____

_____

_____

_____

Ask yourself how these circumstances have shaped your heart and your attitude toward others. It's easy to let pain and sorrow begin to stir up anger inside of us, and like the elder brother, we can quickly get angry at everybody.

If you know you are an angry woman, do whatever it takes to untangle that thread from your life. Life is too short.

If living as the prodigal or the elder brother is long ago in the past or you never chose one of those paths, I praise God on your behalf. You bear no scars and live as a testimony to a life surrendered to God. Celebrate the goodness of God and the power of His grace to keep you from heartache.

DAY 3

A DESPERATE AND PURSUING HEART

We've been talking about hearing God call you beautiful and dancing in His arms. I bet you realize by now that the world isn't really cooperating with this whole idea. If it involves your heart and God, then a battle will likely ensue. The battle is for your soul, and if Satan can't have your soul, he'll settle for ruining your entire life. He'd love for you to be miserable from now until heaven. He'd love for you never to dance. And he'd love for you to keep missing the invitation of God.

What are you going to do about it? Remain the same? Dream about dancing but never really move your feet? I know you're almost too tired to fight. Too old to care so much anymore. And too accustomed to the life you've known to get excited about changing. A friend said to me the other day, "I've already started over twice in my life. I'm 47 years old, and I don't think I have the energy to do it again." I understand, and yet, there is so much left to live. I felt like screaming, "You are too wonderful to quit. Please don't let your heart die this young. There is dancing ahead. God is still on the throne and able to move heaven and earth to redeem your life. Just call His name."

God is still on the throne and able to move heaven and earth to redeem your life. Just call His name.

Every distraction imaginable will come to lure you away from the arms of God. But this is about wanting Him more than you want anything else. There is a conscious choosing ahead. You will have to decide, "Do I want to dance the dance of my life, or do I just want to keep shuffling around?"

I believe these next days of study are pivotal. A hinge, so to speak. If you decide to apply the message of this study to your life, this is the place where you will turn in that direction.

THE CHURCH LADY

I hope I don't offend you with my ideas about "the church lady." Well, maybe I hope I ruffle your feathers a little. I love the church. I grew up in church. I can't remember not being around the church and church gatherings and church people. It just took me way too long to realize that being a "church lady" didn't mean I knew anything about the heart and passion of God.

I grew up going to youth group, potlucks, homecoming, gospel singing under revival tents, committee meetings, bake sales, car washes, retreats, conferences, and any other spiritual-sounding activity that was advertised in the church bulletin. I absolutely loved it. I had a place and felt loved and accepted. I loved the people, the hubbub, and the routine. I was good at doing church.

> What about you? What was your introduction to church? Did you grow up there or come to church later in life?
>
> _____
>
> _____
>
> _____
>
> _____
>
> _____

The church lady has a good heart. She is drawn to God and wants to serve Him out of gratitude. She wants to learn more about the One who has saved her. It's just that over time, more serving and more learning may become a checklist or a substitute for deeper passion ... a *doing* instead of a *becoming*.

Hear my heart. I still love church. I just missed the whole point of God for many years. Somehow I loved becoming the church lady and mistook that for becoming godly. But it feels so good to be in the "church club"—to hang out with your friends, bring food to the sick, make care packages for the refugees, and teach children's church. It can feel so good that it becomes the substitute for a passionate pursuit of God.

Service, giving, and sacrifice are fabulous and a part of the calling for every believer. But *serving* and *doing* do not equal a relationship with God. They don't get us closer to the mark and sometimes become a curtain we hide behind, pretending we know what we're talking about.

Every Sunday morning moms and dads all across the country hand their babies across half doors to the good people who work in the nursery. People serve in a hundred places in the church. They may never make it to the service, but they've "been to church." Some people are hiding in nurseries, classrooms, and kitchens. Some have hidden for years.

How about you? Have you become a church lady? Theologically educated? Hospitable? Quiet and gentle? Hiding and incredibly empty? 🌿 ❏ yes ❏ no 🌿

If so, how did it happen and how does it make you feel?

_____

_____

_____

_____

What avenues have you taken in your walk with Christ that could be labeled "church lady"?

_____

_____

_____

Does it make sense that *doing* is not *becoming*? All of us are *doing* like crazy. Very few of us are *becoming*. My counselor is booked solid with Christian women who are dying on the inside. Service and hospitality are not cutting it. Hearts are broken and lives are hurting, and we just keep signing up for one more thing, hoping we'll stumble into healing and passion.

Who can you tell? When you get the church-lady groove going, it seems as if you have it all together. After a few years of pretending, you decide it's probably better not to find out any different. You meet with other women, but nothing powerful happens because you're all just smiling.

Being the church lady touches my need for a sense of belonging, at least
a pseudo-sense of belonging. I think I found safety in the structure.
—Nancy

Let's talk about small groups—women who meet together for Bible study or prayer or fellowship. I hope you are in one right now.

Write down every good thing you can think of about belonging to a small group of women. _____

_____

_____

_____

_____

What is your heart's desire in regard to a small group? What would your dream group be, and how would you relate to one another?

_____

_____

_____

_____

What are the pitfalls of this kind of connectedness? How have you been burned in the past? What makes you hesitant with these women? _____

_____

_____

_____

THE UNCHURCH LADY

Read that carefully. I'm not talking about becoming an *unchurched* lady, a woman who doesn't make herself a part of the church. I'm talking about becoming the opposite of the church lady I have been.

I wish I could make a quick list—10 easy steps. There is no such list. Becoming unchurch is about laying down pretense and facades. It's about stepping outside the lines you have drawn around your spirituality and seeing what God has for you. He has more for you than you can imagine. If you have wrangled your spirituality into categories with neat little answers for every situation imaginable, then hang on. God is probably getting ready to blow the doors off.

I can't package this idea into some structure where one size fits all. As my pastor would say, this kind of change requires a "paradigm shift." Your framework for thinking and feeling may need demolition and reconstruction. All of

If you have wrangled your

spirituality into categories

with neat little answers

for every situation

imaginable, then hang on.

God is probably getting

ready to blow the doors off.

the strong, essential elements of your faith still there, just rearranged to reflect more clearly the heart of God.

> Sometimes it's easier to remain the church lady because we're afraid of what the unchurch lady might be. Are you afraid?
> ❧ ❑ yes ❑ no ❧
>
> If so, why? _____
> _____
> _____
> _____

I pray that you are feeling the powerful tug of the Holy Spirit. That you sense God calling you toward *becoming* and balancing that call with all the *doing* that can so easily distract. May you desire the passionate life above all else.

DAY 4

DANGEROUS

I have a godly friend who says she wants to become dangerous. Not your typical church-lady aspiration. Some of us might initially think she's stepped across the line of freedom and into rebellion. But God knows her heart. He knows she lived timidly for too many years. He knows she lived under strict interpretations of doctrine that did not reflect the Father's merciful intentions. He knows she desires to glorify Him with every word from her mouth and every step in her journey. I think He loves that she wants to be dangerous. She is saying, "I want to be strong in the name of Jesus. I want wisdom and the courage to take God-sized risks where very few will. I want to speak up in confidence when I have something to say. I want to be vulnerable and transparent. I want my life to draw others into this adventure that is life in Christ."

Come to think of it, she makes me want to be dangerous too.

> What would you look like as an unchurch lady? What would your attributes be? _____
> _____
> _____
>
> Who in your life would be threatened if you became unchurch?
> _____

Does becoming unchurch seem like becoming "unchristian" to you? 🕊 ❑ yes ❑ no 🕊 If yes, what makes you struggle with this idea?_____

_____

_____

Moving from church lady into unchurch lady doesn't happen without a "want to." Most of us try every other spiritual endeavor before we get there. Becoming unchurch requires becoming desperate. Just the thought of it is enough to scare most of us away.

POOR IN SPIRIT

Definition of desperate: Involving or employing extreme measures in an attempt to escape defeat or frustration.

I always thought that desperation was to be avoided at any cost. Now I am learning that being desperate isn't always a reflection of a disaster but an attitude to cultivate. Desperation for God is a good thing.

If you became desperate for God, do you understand what that could mean for the rest of your life? It might mean you get extreme, willing to do anything or fight any battle to escape the pitiful way you have been wandering through life. It means you decide the fight is worth it. Why should frustration and confusion keep winning when life in Christ offers a light for your feet and purpose for your days? To become desperate for God means you begin to live in the victory promised to you in Jesus Christ.

Here is where you will have to turn your life in order to change and become, or you can choose not to turn and remain where you are. The choice is yours. I am fervently praying that you are overcome with great courage and desire. I am asking God to make you hungry for Him, consumed with a craving for His power and passion.

The kingdom of heaven means being near to the presence of God. The presence of God is what you and I have been talking about since the beginning of this study. To be in the presence of God is to be dancing in His arms. That's where the riches of His gifts are. That's where our hearts long to be.

"Blessed are the poor in spirit, For theirs is the kingdom of heaven."

Matthew 5:3 , NKJV

What do you believe the Father has waiting for you in His presence?

_____

What is missing from your life? _____

_____

_____

What does your heart crave? _____

_____

_____

The kingdom, the presence of God, is a blessing that comes to the poor in spirit. Poverty of spirit comes to us after we have tried to do life on our own and realize we cannot be enough.

We have looked inside our souls and seen that nothing good is there. We have owned up to our sin and fessed up to our motives. We have yelled and cursed and screamed. We've finally let the truth of our insides out; into the light comes the reality of poverty.

Understanding our own poverty means we realize that apart from God we cannot do anything purposeful, eternal, good, righteous, or holy. We cannot fill ourselves with achievements. We cannot manipulate relationships to make us whole. We come to see our emptiness for what it truly is: the absence of God.

I have a friend who has been saved and set apart for all eternity. I truly believe she belongs to the Father and, at one point, gave herself to Him fully. Now she walks at a distance. Her life is a mess. Her soul is a mess. She frets and worries like no one else I've ever met. Her relationships at every turn are strained and difficult. Her career is suffering. Her marriage ended three years ago. She is spinning like a top, on the phone all the time with anyone who will listen, e-mailing, whining, becoming more and more the victim of "an awful life."

Right off the bat I knew my place in her life: take her back to Jesus. And I did. And she politely went with me. But she turned right around and wandered away. I was a little dismayed but tried to be faithful. I got right back in there, interacted for days, and took her by the hand back to Jesus. "Stay here and don't move again," I firmly instructed. She nodded her tear-stained face in agreement. She wandered away again. She knows better. She is lost with a map in her pocket. It makes no sense to me. But I finally realized, she's not desperate yet. She feels desperate about her circumstances, but she's not desperate for Jesus. She still thinks she can figure this one out. There is no poverty of spirit about her.

"Without Me you can do nothing."

John 15:5, NKJV

Do you truly realize that apart from Jesus, you can do nothing? ❏ yes ❏ no How do you know this to be true?

_____

_____

How desperate are you? Are you like my friend who keeps wandering in and out of the presence of God, or are you ready to do whatever it takes to get to Him? ❏ I'm still wandering. ❏ I'm ready to do whatever it takes.

If you aren't ready, what will it take to make you crave God?

_____

_____

_____

_____

Are you afraid of being desperate? ❧ ☐ yes ☐ no ❧ If yes, of what are you afraid? _____

_____

_____

_____

I am finding great comfort and peace in my desperateness for God. I feel I finally have the answer that continues to feed my soul.

Write a prayer asking God to make you desperate for His presence.

_____

_____

_____

_____

_____

_____

_____

_____

Picture the scene of starving people in a third world country. Children are dying from malnutrition. Disease is rampant. Day after day, the only task, the only important thing, is finding something to eat or drink. The people are desperate and without any resources of their own.

One day the trucks from a relief organization arrive with fresh water and bags of grain. How do the people respond? Do they stand politely in line with their cup for water and their bucket for grain? Do they politely ask, "May I have some water if it's not too much trouble or if there's any left?" No way. These people are desperate. They are starving. They are hopeless without the supplies. They charge the grain truck. They climb over one another to get the food that will save them. Starving people are not polite and orderly. When you are starving, you are desperate.

Are you ready to charge the grain truck so that you can live the rest of your days in the presence of God? This is the hinge. This is the turn you've been waiting for.

If you are hungry and ready to admit your desperation, sign and date this statement:

I'm ready to do whatever it takes to get to Jesus.

Name: _____

Date: _____

DAY 5

EAT, SLEEP, DRINK, BREATHE

I imagine this is all feeling a little radical to you right now. I hope so. Mediocre hasn't cut it. A casual glance toward God will not fill the emptiness. A Sunday pursuit will leave us feeling indifferent by Tuesday.

I believe we are supposed to live every day in desperate pursuit of the only One who can give the food that will fill our empty souls. I call it learning to eat, sleep, drink, and breathe Jesus.

> How would it look if you decided to eat, sleep, drink, and breathe Jesus? Where would you begin? Think of five areas. Remember, we are charging the grain truck. I want to let you go slowly, but my heart tells me you need to take off running hard and fast after Jesus.
> 1. _____
> 2. _____
> 3. _____
> 4. _____
> 5. _____

This desperate pursuit is more a state of mind than anything else. When you get hungry, the desire for food is consuming. It infiltrates everything you do.

> Anyone who lives on milk, being still an infant, is not acquainted with the teaching about righteousness. But solid food is for the mature, who by constant use have trained themselves to distinguish good from evil. Therefore let us leave the elementary teachings about Christ and go on to maturity.
>
> Hebrews 5:13–6:1

Read the Hebrews passage in the margin and see what happens when we begin to crave spiritual food. In Hebrews 6:1, the writer calls spiritual milk "the elementary teachings about Christ." Based on that definition, how would you define "solid food"?

_____

_____

Who can miss God's teaching about righteousness?

_____

What kind of person will be fed by solid food?

_____

What happens to a person who commits to the constant intake of solid food? _____

_____

What might keep you from remaining desperate for the solid food of God? Think through the obstacles so you can head them off.

_____

_____

_____

_____

_____

> *Actually, I'm afraid of passion, both spiritually with God and physically with my husband.*
>
> —an honest woman

Do you know a woman who is desperate for God? ❏ yes ❏ no
If yes, what is her name and how can you spend time with her?

_____

_____

_____

_____

HIS GREAT DELIGHT

What does God do with a desperate woman? He picks her up into the arms of His presence. He quiets her heart with gentle love songs. He feeds her empty soul with the bounty of His love.

That is exactly where I want to spend my entire life. In the arms of God. I have been a million other places but nothing fills my longing, speaks to every desire, calms my spirit, and gives me courage like the presence of God.

Can you hear God singing over you? Listen to the music of His words from this passage in Song of Songs:

> How beautiful you are, my darling!
>> Oh, how beautiful!
>> Your eyes behind your veil are doves.
>> Your hair is like a flock of goats
>>> descending from Mount Gilead.
> Your teeth are like a flock of sheep just shorn,
>> coming up from the washing.
> Each has its twin;
>> not one of them is alone.
> Your lips are like a scarlet ribbon;
>> your mouth is lovely.
> Your temples behind your veil
>> are like the halves of a pomegranate.

Your neck is like the tower of David,
       built with elegance;
on it hang a thousand shields,
       all of them shields of warriors.
Your two breasts are like two fawns,
       like twin fawns of a gazelle
       that browse among the lilies.
Until the day breaks
       and the shadows flee,
I will go to the mountain of myrrh
       and to the hill of incense.
All beautiful you are, my darling;
       there is no flaw in you.
You have stolen my heart, my sister, my bride;
       you have stolen my heart
with one glance of your eyes,
       with one jewel of your necklace.
How delightful is your love, my sister, my bride!
       How much more pleasing is your love than wine,
       and the fragrance of your perfume than any spice!

Song of Songs 4:1-7,9-10

God sees the desperate woman charging the grain truck and calls her beautiful.

God sees the desperate woman charging the grain truck and calls her beautiful.

If you are still struggling with this truth, write a prayer of longing. If you are beginning to believe the truth of Scripture, write a prayer of gratefulness. _____
_____
_____
_____
_____
_____
_____
_____
_____

I used to have thoughts I wanted to squish because I got so trained as the church lady to cut thoughts off right away. But the desperate woman gives permission to float these thoughts a little longer and ask the Lord what's behind them.

The church lady thinks, "I'm tired," and then gives herself the pat answer, "Do not become weary in doing well." I am learning to let questions rise to the surface and ask Jesus, "Why am I tired, spiritually and emotionally?" I am following a little longer with the thoughts that come to mind.

—Sheila

God sees your emptiness. He knows you can't do this alone. He loves that you have come running to Him, and He calls you beautiful.

NEAR THE KINGDOM

Tell me again, what is the hinge upon which your whole life could turn?

_____

_____

_____

I'm doing the church-lady thing because I don't want to be desperate. I have become fine with serving and working because I'm afraid of the deeper places.

—Lauren

Look around and see if anyone is willing to charge the grain truck with you. There is more strength when we band together. With whom will you go? How will you begin?

_____

_____

_____

_____

_____

_____

_____

_____

_____

I can't wait to meet you and see a new woman, desperate and dancing the dance of her life in the arms of God!

The Only Hope You Have

WEEK 5

Dancing in the arms of God will not insulate us from the winds of the journey or the hurricanes that tear down everything we have built. The only hope we have is Jesus.

The following days of this study are among the first I wrote for the series of *Do You Think I'm Beautiful?* messages. Maybe I wrote these first because they were the most personal and I had to get them out before I could do anything else. Maybe I needed to be reminded where to find my hope before I could begin. Maybe the earth was shaking underneath me in those days, and I had no other option but to write these words.

Being a desperate, free, and passionate woman doesn't guarantee everything will be glorious. It's a real world we dance in, with dangers and enemies and evil lurking. The night we shot the DVD teaching for this week, my mom sat in the audience, just as she had for every other session. For the very first time in front of an audience, I told the difficult story of losing my sister. I never glanced at my mom. I knew I'd lose it if I looked over and saw her broken heart. We lost my sister over 20 years ago. It was an awful hurricane that blew through our lives. Last week my mom was diagnosed with ovarian cancer. The storm has returned with a fury.

We hear God inviting us to dance. The music is wonderful, and we feel beautiful in His arms. Then a big gust of wind blows through our lives and we begin to doubt God. The mountains we built on begin to crumble into the sea. What happened? Where did God go? We thought we were dancing.

This week it will be my privilege to remind you that the only hope we have is Jesus.

VIEWER GUIDE

He ... sends rain on the righteous and the unrighteous.
Matthew 5:45

We are not exempt from the heartache that comes to our humanity.

Mercy doesn't _____.

Mercy doesn't _____.

Mercy lets you know you are being carried through that pain by

_____

When the wind blows, the safest place is _____.

He is an:

_____   _____

_____   _____

_____   _____

and He is coming to the rescue!

God is going to do something ...

you can't even _____.

for the purpose of _____ _____.

so that the _____ you give will be deepened in ways you could not
accomplish on your own.

THE ONLY HOPE
WE HAVE

Memory Verse
Hope does not disappoint us, because God has poured out his love into our hearts by the Holy Spirit, whom he has given us.

Romans 5:5

The LORD is close to the brokenhearted and saves those who are crushed in spirit.

Psalm 34:18

I wish I could tell you that the arms of God would keep you from every awful thing. But Scripture doesn't teach that. I wish I could promise you that grieving and sorrow would not taunt you while He has you. But Scripture says it isn't so. We have the promise of heaven, but until then, this journey, this amazing adventure we live, is beset with trials and weeping that come from a fallen world.

I only know this: In the middle of a great wind, the safest place is deep inside the strongest shelter. When a particularly threatening storm blows into our neighborhood, the authorities advise us to take our families into a room with no windows until danger has passed. Sometimes God asks us to wait in the dark while He protects.

The only safe place we have is the tight embrace of God's love. And the deeper we go, the more we are hidden from destructive winds. Although we do not know what lies ahead, the strength of His protection makes the outcome certain. What may affect you cannot have you. What may wound you cannot destroy you. What may spin you around cannot carry you away. You and I belong to God. He is our certain refuge.

Journal about the storms that have come into your life. Think about the surprise of their arrival, your heart during and after that season, your response to God and others, and lessons you learned.

_____

_____

_____

_____

_____

When my sister died, my daddy told me not to blame myself, but I still did. Is God bringing to mind devastating thoughts or episodes that continue to wander around in your heart? How have you blamed yourself through the years? _____

_____

_____

_____

_____

_____

Are you discovering wounds from the past that have never healed?
◦ ❏ yes   ❏ no ◦ If so, what are they? _____

_____

_____

_____

You can find real shelter in the depth of God's love. Pray and ask Him for that protection.

COMING TO KNOW HIM

How is God filling these roles in your life?

Your Father. "I will be a Father to you, And you shall be My sons and daughters, Says the LORD Almighty" (2 Corinthians 6:18, NKJV).

_____

_____

_____

Your Provider. "Tell them to go after God, who piles on all the riches we could ever manage" (1 Timothy 6:17, THE MESSAGE).

_____

_____

_____

Your Mercy. "In his love and mercy he redeemed them" (Isaiah 63:9).

_____

_____

_____

Your Shelter. "God is a safe place to hide, ready to help when we need him" (Psalm 46:1, THE MESSAGE).

_____

_____

_____

Your Hope. "May the God of hope fill you with all joy and peace as you trust in him, so that you may overflow with hope by the power of the Holy Spirit" (Romans 15:13).

_____

_____

_____

RAIN AND HURRICANES

[God] sends rain on
the righteous and
the unrighteous.

Matthew 5:45

There are no exemptions. Life comes to all of us and one thing is for sure: It just keeps coming, whether we are ready or not.

I don't know what constitutes rain or a hurricane in your life right now, but God does. Sometimes we are suffering the consequences of our choices and sometimes we are suffering just because we are among the living. If rain falls on both the good and the bad, then we must expect to get wet and even drenched sometimes.

Do you sense God speaking to you about any difficulty or sorrow you are facing in your life? ❏ yes ❏ no What is He saying?

_____

_____

_____

Stop and ask for His perspective.

Are you to wait for His rescue? ❏ yes ❏ no Is there a point of action He is prompting you to take? ❏ yes ❏ no If so, what is it? Do you need to involve someone else in the process?

_____

_____

_____

Although we may prefer it, we shall never attain to the fullest fruit-bearing by having all sunshine and no rain. God puts the one over against the other, the dark day of cloud and tempest against the bright day of sunshine and calm—and when the two influences work together in the soul, as they do in the natural world, they produce the greatest degree of fertility and the best condition of heart and life.

—*Charles Spurgeon* [1]

God is our refuge
and strength,
an ever-present
help in trouble.
Therefore we will not
fear, though the earth
give way and the
mountains fall into the
heart of the sea,
though its waters
roar and foam and
the mountains quake
with their surging.

Psalm 46:1-3

WHEN THE FATHER HOLDS YOU IN HIS ARMS

Read Psalm 46:1-3 in the margin. The writer is being pounded by unrelenting wind and rains. Now look at verse 10 in this same chapter: "Be still, and know that I am God."

Sometimes it just gets to be too much. When life seems to be caving in and you know you are in the Father's arms, it's OK to let Him take it for a while. It's OK to allow yourself emotional and physical rest. It's OK to wait for His provision and stop working out your own answer. Hear the Lord say to you, "Rest here in My arms; let Me take this now."

Sometimes we hide in our homes, run away from relationships, or stop interacting or participating in life until the storm passes. Sometimes we have to pull away to regain our senses. But most often I meet women who truly need a refuge for soul rest and restoration. Their souls need to be tended. Their wounds need time to heal. They need to laugh and be distracted more often. Are you one of those women?

I suggest you plan a personal retreat. Don't write me off before you even think about it. Mark the days on the calendar. Use some money or no money. Involve friends or go by yourself. Get away. One night won't really do it: two is better, and three is better still. I could tell you how, but it wouldn't fit your life, so be creative. Get serious about getting away for a few days for your soul.

Use the space below to brainstorm and make plans for your personal retreat.

My target date:_____

Will I go alone or take friends? ❏ go alone ❏ take friends

If I take friends, who will go with me? _____
_____

Where will I go to rest? _____

Possible obstacles and solutions for those obstacles:

Obstacles	Solutions
_____	_____
_____	_____
_____	_____
_____	_____
_____	_____

Three reasons I will be better for indulging in a personal retreat:
1. _____
2. _____
3. _____

Tomorrow we'll pick back up with making plans for you to refresh and refill your soul.

THE FATHER HOLDS
YOU STILL

Yesterday I asked you to plan a personal retreat. I hope you didn't skip over that. I am praying you already have a date blocked on your calendar. The rewards to you and your family will be astounding. You are not superwoman. You are just a woman who needs her God and the soul care that is necessary to deepen your walk with Him.

A second aspect of refilling and restoration is soul refreshment. Look around at your relationships, especially those with your family, and decide who needs to see you look into their eyes. As women, we get a certain amount of comfort and rest from pouring ourselves into the lives of those we love. When I have only been "maintaining" my family, I feel given out and scattered. When I have determined to give in a fresh and conscious way, I feel revived. Significant refreshment comes from turning away from the hurricane and giving out love. It is a conscious effort to stop doing and to take a few moments to give of yourself. In giving there is abundant receiving.

Who needs a little more of you right now? _____

_____

What could you give? _____

_____

How do you think God will fill you as you decide to give?

_____

_____

_____

Third, refill and restore by laughing more. Most of our lives are no laughing matter. Hurricanes are serious and devastating. But find someone who makes you laugh and stand around that person. People laugh because they have given themselves permission to enjoy humor. It's good for your soul to enjoy a silly joke or funny story. Do you remember the last time you laughed until you cried? How long has it been? Give yourself permission to enjoy and laugh again. Watch what happens in your heart and watch how people are drawn into your delight.

In what other ways is God directing you to care for your soul in this season of life? _____

_____

_____

No matter where you find yourself or what storm may be raging in your life, God's directive to us is, "Be still." Do not fret and wring your hands with worry. Lean deeper into Him and feel His strength.

How is God trying to speak to you? Have you been still enough to hear His strong voice? Settle yourself in these next moments; listen to Him speak. What is He saying?

_____

_____

_____

MY DELIVERER

I was listening to a radio talk show one afternoon and a man was talking about the impending nuclear war, the effects of biological warfare, the depravity of evildoers who desire to bring death and destruction to people all over the world. I kept listening, even though everything in me wanted to turn it off. The discussion made me have that deep sinking feeling in the pit of my stomach.

At the end of the show, the host asked his guest, "As believers, what can we do? This is all rather scary." I agreed and waited for an answer. The guest replied, "The only hope we have is the only hope we've ever had. We've never had another option apart from God, and nothing is different now. He is our Hope. He has provided our Savior." Immediately, my soul found rest. How quickly I had forgotten: I belong to God.

"The only hope we have is the only hope we've ever had."

No matter what your circumstances today, you belong to God Almighty! He is your invincible Warrior. Your fearless Protector. Your merciful Father. He will fight for you. He is not afraid of anything or anybody. He is the One who speaks and stills storms. Is your hope all gone? God is the only hope you've ever had.

Read from your Bible about our Deliverer in Exodus 14.

When the Israelites were up against the Red Sea with the Egyptians at their backs, they decided they'd rather go back to bondage because they could not see what God was going to do.

Have you ever wanted to go back to your old life or your old patterns of bondage just because you couldn't figure things out on your own? ❧ ❏ yes ❏ no ❧

What did you do with those fears and desires? _____
_____
_____

Are you in the dark right now, waiting for a storm to pass, wondering where God is? Claim Him as your Deliverer. Find renewed strength in knowing that He comes to the rescue. Trust that He will show up in glory to fight for you.

Journal your prayer. _____
_____
_____
_____
_____
_____
_____
_____
_____
_____

BE STILL AND WATCH

God wants you and me to be still and watch, because He wants us to see His great power. When we see the power of God at work in our lives, we learn to trust Him more. We learn to lean in closer. We learn to wait in the dark patiently. We learn that our God is really who He claims to be. We learn that He is truly our only hope.

Do you trust God:
with your circumstances? ❧ ❏ yes ❏ no ❧
with your difficulties? ❧ ❏ yes ❏ no ❧
with your grief? ❧ ❏ yes ❏ no ❧

With what or for what are you trusting God? _____
_____

How can you more effectively live in the power of trust?
_____
_____
_____

What would that look like in your life? _____

_____

_____

Where could fretting be reduced and worry be replaced?

_____

_____

If you are strong one day and weak the next, do not give up. Claim again the truth of Scripture. God is your Deliverer. God is your only hope. God is coming in glory to calm the winds and make a way.

D A Y   3

HIS PERFECT LOVE

In these next days, I want us to begin looking at the woman who *knows* God calls her beautiful. What does she look like? What does she sound like? What difference does it make to be dancing in His arms? What can you expect to happen as you lean into the truths of God's wild love for you?

Many of us are laden with fears. I hope in these next pages we can understand and apply the answer that removes fear—being fully formed in God's perfect love. A woman who knows God calls her beautiful is moving away from a life of fear and running toward the strength that comes from perfect love. She is being renewed in purpose and in vision. She is waking up to life and trusting in the hope God has set within her.

I am excited about this part of our journey. I am eagerly anticipating the work of God in your life. What if these thoughts really connect with your spirit and you hear the voice of God gently speak, "I have so much more for you"? First it could be little steps and then a freedom to run as you never have before.

A woman who knows God calls her beautiful is running toward the strength that comes from perfect love.

Am I Tied On?

I heard a story about a man who works at a bungee jump. He stands on a platform, paid to carefully strap in those who want to step over into nothing, scream with fear, lose their breath, bounce upside down, and dangle. He wears a T-shirt that reads, "Shut Up and Jump."

I told my seminary mentor and friend, Dennis, that story and then added, "I need a T-shirt like his. I am standing on a platform scared to death, afraid to jump, and ready to chat. I'm all talk and no jump. As a matter of fact, I would rather talk about anything than jump … 50 ways to jump, 50 ways not to jump, velocity, wind speed, appropriate jumping attire, other people who have jumped before me—anything to avoid my fears."

We laughed and then Dennis said, "Tell me why you're so afraid."

"I don't know exactly. Maybe I'm afraid I'm not tied on. Tied on to God."

My seminary mentor sighed patiently and then said, "Angela, you are more tied on than you know. Maybe you know it in that head of yours, but you have forgotten with your heart."

"Dennis, what if I make a mistake?"

"Even if you make a mistake, God still has you."

"And my children?"

"He has them too. You are tied on with a bond that cannot be broken. And when you are tied on to God, you do not have to be afraid."

"When you are tied on to God, you do not have to be afraid."

Remembering the bungee worker always makes me laugh at the thought of the T-shirt. But the truth of Dennis' words always call me toward reflection.

When I think about talking instead of jumping, I try to take a quick life inventory: Where am I all talk and no jump? Where am I dreaming but not pursuing? Why am I afraid? What steps can I take to counter a paralyzing fear?

Have you ever bungee jumped or parachuted from a plane?
❏ yes ❏ no If you have, describe how it feels to be falling and then caught. If not, describe how you imagine it would feel.

_____

_____

_____

Does your life ever give you the same emotions? ❏ yes ❏ no
If so, how? _____

_____

How do you react when life pulls one of those loop de loops just as you thought things were coasting? Do you react with trust or find yourself worried and fearful? _____

_____

_____

Is anything in your life requiring you to jump into the realm of the unknown? ❏ yes ❏ no If so, what is it? _____

_____

_____

Is there a place where you are sitting in the dark and waiting?
❧ ❑ yes ❑ no ❧ Where is the place? Describe the dark and the
waiting. _____
_____
_____

Do you feel as if you have been thrown from a train and told to find
your own way home? ❧ ❑ yes ❑ no ❧ How or why?
_____
_____
_____

For these reasons or a hundred others, you could be wrestling with our archenemy called Fear.

Which statement best reflects where Fear is abiding in your life
right now?
❑ There is no Fear in my home. He has been kicked out and
    banned from the property.
❑ He is standing at the front door knocking.
❑ I let Fear in the house, but we are only visiting in the foyer.
❑ Fear has stayed for dinner.
❑ I am tucked underneath my cozy blankets with Fear snuggled up
    beside me.

If you knew God was calling you to free-fall into an adventure He
has planned for you, what would your resistance be? _____
_____
_____

Do you second-guess His voice? ❧ ❑ yes ❑ no ❧ How?
_____
_____

Do you wonder if you are truly tied on to God? ❧ ❑ yes ❑ no ❧
What makes you wonder? _____
_____
_____

Do you still question why God would want to catch a woman like
you? ❧ ❑ yes ❑ no ❧ What makes you question?
_____
_____

GOD met me more
than halfway,
he freed me from
my anxious fears.

Psalm 34:4, THE MESSAGE

If the only way to conquer fear is to jump anyway, then how do you get there? First, you have to know if you are on the right platform. Are you where God wants you? Are you pursuing His heart of love for you? Have you been still enough to listen for His voice?

Second, recheck the security of your straps. Do others confirm your pursuits or give you warnings? Are you convinced in your heart that you are tied on to the unrelenting love of God? Do you live your life like that? Do you live strong and assured of His presence or weak and doubting His role in your life?

Even if you make a mistake, you still belong to God. He can reel you back in and redirect your path.

If you are living in the wake of a huge mistake, take a few minutes to journal where you are, how you got there, and your desire to know that God still has you._____

_____

_____

_____

_____

_____

_____

_____

DAY 4

THE WEAK-WILLED WOMAN

They are the kind who
worm their way into
homes and gain control
over weak-willed women,
who are loaded down
with sins and are swayed
by all kinds of evil
desires, always learn-
ing but never able to
acknowledge the truth.

2 Timothy 3:6-7

Read 2 Timothy 3:6-7 in the margin and see these words with your own eyes. *Weak-willed women.* How can I read my Bible for years and miss stuff like that? I probably always thought Paul was talking about someone else, women back in Bible days, not me. It makes me cringe to think I could have "weak-willed" potential. Actually, it kind of makes me angry. But I must set aside the temptation to be insulted and examine my own heart for truth. Have I ever been weak-willed? Yes. Do I want to live like that? Absolutely not.

This portion of our study might be painful. If some of this applies to you, it's not going to feel great when it lands. So prepare your heart and mind to receive truth. Pray about laying aside any predisposition to ignore the promptings of the Holy Spirit. If you get your feelings hurt or begin to feel a twinge of anger, stop and ask God what's going on in your heart. Make sure you find out what He's trying to say to you.

Read 2 Timothy 3:1-5. While you are reading, do a little soul-searching and ask yourself if there are traces of these forms of godlessness in your life. I have duplicated Paul's list below. If some hit closer to home for you, write your thoughts on the lines below.

lovers of themselves	lovers of money	boastful
proud	abusive	ungrateful
unholy	without love	disobedient to parents
unforgiving	slanderous	brutal
without self-control	treacherous	not lovers of the good
rash	conceited	

lovers of pleasure rather than lovers of God

having a form of godliness but denying its power

_____

_____

_____

_____

_____

_____

Don't miss what Paul says at the end of this list concerning the godless: "Have nothing to do with them" (v. 5).

If it's true that women can be weak-willed, then it is also true that I have weak-willed potential. Eugene Peterson translated those words as "unstable and needy." The truth is, women can be fairly easily given over to "unstable and needy" tendencies.

Let me describe a weak-willed woman to you. Consider the characteristics in regard to your own life. If you need to take some medicine, hold your nose and gag it down. We're trying to get healthy, and sometimes taking bad-tasting medicine will do that. Check all the characteristics that apply to you.

The weak-willed woman can be:
❑ consumed with her fears.
❑ self-absorbed.
❑ caring too much about appearances and what everyone else thinks.
❑ an invisible, frightened church mouse.

❑ loud, brash, and dominant.

❑ empty of ambition and passion.

❑ controlling.

❑ deaf to the voice of God, never hearing Him call her beautiful.

❑ full of self-pity.

❑ defeated by depression.

❑ harboring a grudge.

❑ prone to gossip.

❑ indulging her obsessions.

❑ easily hurt or offended.

❑ spiritually knowledgeable but essentially without discernment.

❑ attending church and Bible studies but never changing or growing.

❑ given to a critical spirit.

Did you see anything of yourself here? If it is something very small, or if it is volumes, begin a prayer of transparent confession to God.

These struggles of our flesh are not just little sins to be dealt with. This passage says that any form of godlessness is a foothold for our enemy to work his way into our lives. He wants to scare you to death, beat you down, and keep you afraid.

The reasoning is almost circular. We can become weak-willed because of our fears. And then fear can quickly feed our weak-willed potential. The result either way is a very fragile woman.

What do you think you're afraid of? Answer the following questions.

Are you afraid of change? ❑ yes ❑ no Why? _____

_____

_____

_____

To confidently anticipate that change will continue to come toward us is to move out of the shadows of great fear and into the light of expectancy.

Do you fear heartache, pain, and suffering? ❑ yes ❑ no

If so, in what ways? _____

_____

_____

The insulated life does not exist. Even the woman who seems to have it all together and seems to have every material blessing walks the same path we do—one fraught with twists and turns

Say to them that are of a fearful heart, Be strong, fear not: behold, your God will come ... he will come and save you.

Isaiah 35:4, KJV

of heartache where she can be ambushed by the bully of suffering. If we could understand that there are no suffering exemptions for the living, maybe we would not give our minds over to such depths of worry and fear.

Are you afraid of loneliness? ❧ ❑ yes ❑ no ❧ Why? _____
_____

We won't have some elements of relationship with Jesus until we step into His presence in heaven. But He can still provide. Tell Him about your fears and ask Him to fight this one for you. Entrust Him with your heart. Be honest about the depth of your desire, but don't hide. Hiding feeds the fear of loneliness. Step out into the light and watch Him come to provide. He delivers kisses and hugs in the most delightful ways. He directs angels to make phone calls and write notes. Wait right there in His presence and see how He comes to provide.

The LORD is close to
 the brokenhearted
and saves those who
are crushed in spirit.

Psalm 34:18

Do you fear failure? ❧ ❑ yes ❑ no ❧ If so, in what ways?
_____
_____

Failure is not dying. Failure is not the end unless it keeps us from trying again. Maybe instead of failure, we'd do better to fear the death of dreaming.

Do you fear disappointment? ❧ ❑ yes ❑ no ❧ How does it make you afraid? _____
_____
_____

The archenemy of hope is the fear of disappointment. It tethers our celebration. It tempers our praise. We hold on and hold back, afraid to get too excited about anything.

Do you live in fear of being rejected? ❧ ❑ yes ❑ no ❧
By whom? _____

Country music songwriters would have little to write about apart from the severe suffering that comes from unrequited love and refusal. And their music wouldn't be so popular if the ache weren't universal.

I have been the weak-willed woman. Maybe you have been too. It breaks my heart to remember how often I have lived and made decisions from my fears. But good news is coming tomorrow! Let God deal with the truth of our weakness today and then anticipate His perfect love coming with glory in the morning.

DAY 5

IN THE SAME ROOM AS LOVE

Remember the weak-willed woman from yesterday's study? The woman you and I have the potential to become? She has been mocked by the bully of fear. The bully pushes, ridicules, and provokes until the weak-willed woman comes undone from her consequences, heartache, and pain.

I am 52 and a "weak-willed woman." I have carried fear around with me for years. It goes to work with me. It stands beside me when I talk to the children. It laughs at me when my husband isn't home on time and I want to get in the car and drive past her house. How I hate this knot in my stomach. I want to be in love with God and have my girls see that love in me. I don't want to be weak-willed anymore.

—Shirley

Fear is our enemy. It is like a bully that keeps coming around to pester, provoke, and hurt. Living in the same room as Fear will make us incredibly weak-willed women. The bully called Fear might always get the best of us except for one thing—we have a Friend who is bigger than Fear. We have a Lover who comes to our rescue. Because we belong to God Almighty, we have not been left alone in a back alley with a bully.

Underline words in the passage below that speak to your heart.

God is love. Whoever lives in love lives in God, and God in him. In this way, love is made complete among us so that we will have confidence on the day of judgment, because in this world we are like him. There is no fear in love. But perfect love drives out fear, because fear has to do with punishment. The one who fears is not made perfect in love.

1 John 4:16-18

According to this passage, what makes you complete?

_____

What character trait comes from being made complete by the love of God? _____

Following is my very loose paraphrase of this passage according to the themes we've been discussing.

> *God is love. The woman who dances in the arms of God has God's love in her. God's love fills the whole room so there are no shadows where bullies can hide. God's love gives a woman righteous confidence. He loves her like He loves Christ, and that should take away all her worries about Judgment Day. There is no place for fear in the same room as love. Perfect Love chases away the bullies of fear because all they want to do is make you believe you deserve punishment. The woman who fears is not dancing in the arms of Perfect Love.*

Which statement is true?
- ❏ I can drive away my fears if I just try hard enough.
- ❏ I will never live without fear; it's a part of being alive.
- ❏ God, who is Perfect Love, can come and completely drive out all my fear.

We all struggle with some of the following. Read the Scriptures referenced and describe how each passage helps us to combat that fear.

"God can't really love me." Romans 8:38-39

_____

_____

"I'm not special." Psalm 139:13-16

_____

_____

"I'm afraid of rejection." Galatians 1:10

_____

_____

"I can't measure up." Colossians 1:21-22

_____

_____

The same God who has asked us to dance—the One who calls us beautiful —is called Perfect Love.

The same God who has asked us to dance—the One who calls us beautiful—is called Perfect Love. And where we are fully formed in the perfect love of God, there will be no fear. Fear cannot be in the same room as Perfect Love. There is One who does battle with the bully. There is a Rescuer ready to hear your cries of weakness and fear.

Do you hear the bully trying to heckle you even now? He may be saying things like: "Don't believe any of this mumbo jumbo." "This doesn't really apply to you." "God is not coming to your rescue."

When you are being heckled, run into the presence of God and pray for His deliverance. How are you learning to get into the presence of God? _____

_____

_____

In 1 John 4:18, John said, "Fear has to do with punishment." We remain in our fears because we believe we deserve punishment. For what do you believe you should continue to be punished?

_____

_____

There is now no condemnation for those who are in Christ Jesus.

Romans 8:1

In Jesus there is no condemnation. Because of the blood of Jesus, because of His death on the cross, there has already been enough punishment. When we say we believe Jesus is the Son of God and understand that His death was enough to pay for our sins, then we have been covered. According to God, we have then been given the same position as Christ, the blessing of being called His daughter.

If you believe you still deserve more punishment, then you are not fully leaning into this truth of Scripture. Put your weight into it and believe it. Jesus has already done enough. Accept it and rest. According to Galatians 5:1, God has set you free so that you can be free indeed. No more punishment necessary.

I have been afraid for so long, but I do not want to be afraid anymore. Some of my greatest spiritual battles have been in regard to overcoming fear. These battles are intense and they can scorch the soul. Their cinders reignite long after I think the fire has been put out. I can once again listen to the bully I thought I'd forgotten. When I feel the bully yank my hair or hear him heckle me from the front row, I am learning to run with everything I have into the presence of God.

I fall on my face and lie on my floor and pray desperate prayers:

God, rescue me from the bully. God, come quickly; I do not want to be taunted today. God, send angels to cover me with their protection. God, let me believe Your truth instead of the

lies. Stand me up in strength with renewed courage and power.
Go before me. Hold me. Defend me.

The power of a bully is neutralized when we quit believing him. We don't want to spend any more days in the grip of his deceit and confusion.

Do you realize what kind of woman you might be without your fears? Try to envision yourself without fear. You will be amazing!

The thing I would most like to do if I could overcome my fear is:

_____

_____

One thing I used to be afraid of but no long am is:

_____

I think I'm afraid of _____

because of _____.

The bravest woman I know is _____

I have never been afraid to _____

because _____.

If I could sit down and talk to Jesus face to face about my fears, I would tell Him _____

_____

_____

_____

_____

Do you hear the tender voice of God calling to you? Could He be saying, "I have been dreaming of you without fear. Those aspirations are the ones I gave to you. I have you. You are tied on. Even if you make a mistake, I promise I'll catch you. You belong to Me. It's OK. Now shut up and jump"?

Maybe you have been the weak-willed woman, taunted by the bully of fear. But you can rejoice. Perfect Love has come to the rescue.

---

1. C.H. Spurgeon, "Clear Shining After Rain," Spurgeon Gems, *http://www.spurgeongems.org/vols37-39/chs2284.pdf* (accessed May 22, 2007).

A Beautiful Crown

WEEK 6

God is enthralled by the beauty of a woman and calls her His beloved. He wildly pursues her heart with romance and intimacy to make her His beautiful bride.

We are still talking about what a woman looks like when she comes to believe God calls her beautiful. One honest comment I hear when I speak on this topic is: "Angela, I hear you. I see God's answer in Scripture. It makes sense. But I am having a hard time believing it for myself. I can't believe God sees all of me and calls me beautiful."

This is a spiritual battle. Satan knows what kind of woman you could become if you began to live out the truths we've been discussing. He doesn't want you ever to believe God calls you beautiful. He is the accuser of believers, and he never gives up. The more you discover about the heart of God, the louder Satan shouts, "It's not so."

He knows all your weak places and presses into them. He doesn't want you to get this. He knows how much more passionate and purposeful your life will be in the arms of God.

If something is keeping you from applying these truths, if you continue to stand back and question the depth of God's love, then maybe you have inclined your ear toward the Accuser. Maybe he is playing with your head. And I'm sure he's pleased that you drag your heart around, making excuses, staying too busy or distracted.

The whole idea of our spiritual journey is that we be changed into God's likeness. The Accuser wants you to stay the same and even spiral toward emotional death. Will you fight? Your life is too precious and the potential too great. Decide you will do whatever it takes to walk in the truth of God's love. He really does call you beautiful. Live like a woman who knows it's true!

VIEWER GUIDE

"The Spirit of the Sovereign LORD is on me,
because the LORD has anointed me
to preach good news to the poor.
He has sent me to bind up the brokenhearted,
to proclaim freedom for the captives
and release from darkness for the prisoners,
to proclaim the year of the LORD's favor
and the day of vengeance of our God,
to comfort all who mourn,
and provide for those who grieve in Zion—
to bestow on them a crown of beauty
instead of ashes,
the oil of gladness
instead of mourning,
and a garment of praise
instead of a spirit of despair.
They will be called oaks of righteousness,
a planting of the LORD
for the display of his splendor."

Isaiah 61:1-3

God takes our _____ and does something with them that we could not have even imagined.

God promises He will replace our ashes with _____.

When the woman who wears a crown of beauty walks in the room, _____

_____ walks in right in front of her.

The Beholder calls you _____ — and it's true!

D A Y   I

MAKING A TRADE

Memory Verse

As a bridegroom
rejoices over his bride,
so will your God
rejoice over you.

Isaiah 62:5

I hope that while you have been doing this study you have been taking note of women who seem to be dancing in the arms of God. Maybe someone you hadn't even expected to notice now seems to be dancing.

What is different about these dancing women? What do others find attractive about them? _____

_____

_____

_____

_____

_____

How do they inspire you? _____

_____

_____

_____

_____

WEEKENDS WITH WOMEN

What was your favorite time away with women? A retreat? Mother/daughter outing? Girls' weekend away? _____

_____

_____

What is your most special memory from that time?

_____

_____

_____

_____

Why? _____

_____

Have you ever had a time away that you would consider life-changing? ❧ ❑ yes ❑ no ❧ If so, describe it. _____

_____

_____

_____

Are you becoming more Christlike? If the question seems too nebulous, consider the following scriptural guidelines:

1. Are you letting go of old ways of acting? "Everything … connected with that old way of life has to go. It's rotten through and through. Get rid of it!" (Ephesians 4:22, THE MESSAGE).
2. Are you changing the way you think? "Let the Spirit change your way of thinking" (Ephesians 4:23, CEV).
3. Are you developing new Christlike habits? "Put on the new self, created to be like God in true righteousness and holiness" (Ephesians 4:24).

> As you look back through your life, what are some of the most significant "life-changing" events, decisions, or encounters?
> _____
> _____
> _____
> _____
>
> Have you been willing or hesitant to change through the years?
> ❏ willing ❏ hesitant   Why? _____
> _____
>
> Do you feel you have continued to improve in the past five years?
> ❏ yes ❏ no
>
> Do you think you look more like Jesus than you used to?
> ❏ yes ❏ no

After pretending to be someone else for so long, I'm now able to love myself for who I am and who God says I am in Christ.

—a woman who is wearing the crown

At many conferences, the last session will be slated for sharing. Women will stand up at the end and tell others what God has been doing in their lives. Many times this session will begin with timidity and end up lasting a couple of hours. Most of the time, the same theme becomes apparent—women tell their stories, but it usually turns out to be a testimony of the God who replaces the ashes of broken lives with crowns of beauty.

Beauty for ashes. What a trade. Only a God who's wildly in love would make a bargain like that.

> If you were standing at a microphone to tell what God is doing in your heart and life, what would you say? _____
> _____
> _____
> _____
> _____

How is God trading your ashes for beauty? _____

_____

_____

_____

_____

THE ASH HEAP

Heart-shattered lives
ready for love
don't for a moment
escape God's notice.

Psalm 51:17, The MESSAGE

When a woman starts believing that God calls her beautiful, amazing things can happen. She really changes, and people begin to notice. In His arms she finds hope, strength, and freedom.

Think about being free from the sack of ashes that has come to you through the difficulties of life. Because you are dancing in the arms of God, you don't have to haul that thing around anymore. He wants to make a trade. He'd like to take away your ashes and see you wearing a crown of beauty.

If you could look into your sack of ashes, what would you see?

_____

_____

_____

Have you decided some things will never heal? some hurts will never go away? some struggles will never end? you'll have to carry them around forever? ❧ ❑ yes ❑ no ❧ If yes, what are they?

_____

_____

Are you sitting in the ashes of a disappointing life? poor choices? guilt, pain, or suffering? Have you taught yourself to go numb so you can't feel the great weight of the ashes? Come to God and decide that you are going to untie the sack of your ashes and pour them out.

When I finally made the decision to pour out my ashes, I began to feel again; everything had to get out. I called my prayer *the outpouring*. I ended up spending days writing the outpouring.

Can you begin to write or pray about the ashes inside of you that need to be poured out? ❧ ❑ yes ❑ not yet ❧ Give it a try.

_____

_____

_____

_____

_____

Maybe this doesn't make any sense to you. Maybe great pain or
sorrow has never come to you. If that is the case, write a prayer of
thanksgiving to God. _____

_____

_____

_____

_____

_____

_____

BINDING THE BROKENHEARTED

Sometimes we convince ourselves that because of our brokenness, we deserve
the labels others give us. Sometimes we get tired and decide this is the way
life is always going to be. I have a friend who recently divorced and almost
threw away her spiritual life after the process. Believing that she had miserably
disappointed God, with those thoughts reinforced by close friends and family,
she decided there was no use in trying anymore. She almost turned away from
God because she believed He could never have anything to do with her again.

Many of us can come to believe we must be second or third choice in God's
eyes because of our scars. I love Micah 7:18: "You … delight to show mercy."

I don't think many of us have heard or applied this truth. Yes, sin is wrong.
Yes, we can make awful mistakes that disappoint God. Yes, there will always be
consequences for willful disobedience. But God delights to show mercy.

Why does it take so long to cry out for mercy? Maybe because we keep tell-
ing ourselves we don't deserve it. But that is the whole point of mercy, isn't it?

Mercy: not getting what I deserve.

Have you asked God for mercy in regard to your sack of ashes—
your brokenness, your pain, and your sorrows? Spend some time
with Him now. Ask Him for the mercy that covers every disappointment and heals every wound.

Turn in your Bible to Isaiah 61:1-3. Read these verses and underline
as God speaks to you. This passage refers to the work of Jesus in
our lives. We'll walk through these verses step-by-step and discover
what mercy God has for us.

> *The Spirit of the Sovereign LORD is on me,*
> *because the LORD has anointed me to preach*
> *good news to the poor. He has sent me to bind*
> *up the brokenhearted (v. 1).*

Jesus our Messiah has been sent to reach us with the good news of God's grace and mercy. He has come to bind up the brokenhearted.

I find great relief in those words. I love that I don't have to figure out how to heal my own broken heart. Jesus willingly and lovingly comes to do that.

Do you have a broken heart that needs mending? ✍ ❑ yes ❑ no ✍ How did these broken places come to you? Journal the journey. Ask God for His mercy that binds broken things. _____

_____

_____

_____

_____

_____

_____

To proclaim freedom for the captives (v. 1).

Jesus is waiting with freedom where you have been held captive. Are there relationships that hold you captive? habits that have become unhealthy and distracting? obsessions? addictions? Maybe you are held captive by your own thoughts. You assume you don't deserve freedom. You relegate yourself to wallflower status. You are afraid you'll fail at freedom.

Where are you being held captive? _____

_____

_____

_____

Ask yourself if you are afraid of freedom. What would you do if you were no longer in bondage? Would you know how to rejoice over your release? _____

_____

_____

_____

_____

_____

_____

_____

Trading in your ashes is a very big deal. We'll pick up here tomorrow.

DAY 2

GOD'S HOLY EXCHANGE

We left off yesterday in Isaiah 61. God is coming to bind up our broken hearts to make righteous and holy exchanges. Let's jump right back in.

> *And release from darkness for the prisoners (v. 1).*

Jesus uses the themes of light and darkness many times in the Gospels. To walk with Him and trust in His Word is to walk in the light. To be apart from His fellowship is to remain in darkness. The holy exchange is to trade in your darkness for light.

Where is darkness still in your life? _____
_____
_____

Jesus wants to offer His light into your darkest place. Ask Him now.

> *To proclaim the year of the LORD's favor*
> > *and the day of vengeance of our God,*
> *to comfort all who mourn (v. 2).*

Our God truly wants to give you comfort where you mourn. He cares about every pain and suffering you have known. He aches with you in loss and grief. Maybe you need to sense the real comfort of God.

Sometimes when I am praying for comfort, I lie on my face in my bedroom or even in my closet and wait. I wait until He really gives comfort. I wait for my heart to be stilled and my countenance to be changed by His presence. When you pray you may need to wait quietly and even longer than you anticipated until God shows up with the comfort you have been looking for.

> *And provide for those who grieve in Zion—*
> *to bestow on them a crown of beauty instead of ashes (v. 3).*

The mercy of God wants to come and take away the cinders of your pain. This is not a one-time life event. God promises to keep coming for your ashes until you stand with Him in heaven, where the crown of beauty is finally eternal. Even though you may be reluctant to ask, Jesus still replaces ashes with beauty. Ask Him. Remember, He delights in your asking and He delights in giving the mercy of beauty!

The oil of gladness
instead of mourning (v. 3).

Believers are not required to live underneath ashes and mourning. There will be seasons in all of our lives, but God comes and makes His holy exchange. Isn't it time to replace your mourning? Isn't it time you asked God for His gladness? Not the church-lady kind of gladness, but the real deal. The kind that comes from your soul.

And a garment of praise
instead of a spirit of despair (v. 3).

My friend Nicole wrote an amazing sketch about breast cancer. It is called "Stepping into the Ring." [1] The idea of the drama is a woman's struggle with despair in the face of devastating news. The first time I watched Nicole's performance, I doubled over with sobs of grief and pain. It can be breast cancer that brings despair, but it can also be a hundred other battles such as divorce, the loss of a child, bankruptcy, other diseases, and on and on.

No wonder so many of us don't even know if we'll make it. The burdens are great. The load is heavy. And yet, for the believer, Jesus offers what we can't even conceive: a garment of praise. Praise comes to our hearts only as we allow Him to trade our despair for His hope.

Have you fallen into a spirit of despair? Do you need the hope of Jesus? He can give it. The Son of God can give you and me a renewed hope that becomes a garment of praise.

> What is your despair? Write about your despairing heart here and ask Jesus for renewed hope and praise. _____
> _____
> _____
> _____
> _____

They will be called oaks of righteousness,
a planting of the LORD
for the display of his splendor (v. 3).

Here is the woman I desire to be. Here is the direction I feel God turning us. A brokenhearted captive who has been sitting in the dark with the pain of her ashes, mourning until she has fallen into despair, can become a display of His splendor!

How? It can happen because God delights to show mercy.

Think about that woman underneath the crown of beauty, the one who has been set free, the one who has traded despair for praise. Now think about yourself. What characteristics do you desire so that you might become an "oak of righteousness," a "display of his splendor"?

Describe the woman you want to become. _____
_____
_____
_____
_____
_____
_____

What would you look like if God literally applied each of these verses to your life? _____
_____
_____
_____

What would you do as that new woman? Have fun with this one. Dream the woman that God is dreaming in you. _____
_____
_____
_____
_____
_____
_____
_____

MORE THAN WE DESERVE

Redemption is when God takes something that seems to have no value or even seems to be a liability and exchanges it for something beautiful.

To receive a vase of flowers in exchange for a paper coupon seems like more than we deserve. To become a woman of righteousness and splendor after a lifetime of defeats, scars, and sin seems impossible and beyond anything we could ever deserve.

We have arrived at one of the most astounding characteristics of God. He always does more than we deserve. Our God is a redeeming God. He willingly takes a sack of ashes in exchange for a crown of beauty. It doesn't make sense. I don't get it. But I am incredibly grateful for the truth of God's amazing love for us.

Redemption is when God takes something that seems to have no value and exchanges it for something beautiful.

Have mercy on me, O God, according to your unfailing love; according to your great compassion blot out my transgressions. Wash away all my iniquity and cleanse me from my sin. For I know my transgressions, and my sin is always before me. Against you, you only, have I sinned and done what is evil in your sight, so that you are proved right when you speak and justified when you judge. Surely I was sinful at birth, sinful from the time my mother conceived me. Surely you desire truth in the inner parts; you teach me wisdom in the inmost place. Cleanse me with hyssop, and I will be clean; wash me, and I will be whiter than snow. Let me hear joy and gladness; let the bones you have crushed rejoice. Hide your face from my sins and blot out all my iniquity. Create in me a pure heart, O God, and renew a steadfast spirit within me. Do not cast me from your presence or take your Holy Spirit from me. Restore to me the joy of your salvation and grant me a willing spirit, to sustain me.

Psalm 51:1-12

What beliefs, patterns, or choices do you need God to redeem?

_____
_____
_____
_____

Gifts that we don't deserve are called *grace*. Accept His willingness to exchange His good for your weakness as a gift of grace. Stop trying to deserve God and just receive His goodness and mercy.

Ask God to make the trade, His beauty for your ashes.

_____
_____
_____
_____
_____
_____

D A Y   3

ALL OF ME

If in the last few pages you have begun to open your soul, I want to encourage you to go ahead and show God everything. When a season of redeeming and mercy came for me, I knew I wanted God to have all of me. I wanted to show Him every flaw, every sin, and every temptation I had been reluctant to deal with. He already knew, but I had never wanted to own up to Him.

I had been great at skipping around my sin and woundedness in my prayer life. I'd rather pray for the missionaries in Siberia than 'fess up to my shortcomings and flaws. Then one day, while my soul was ripped open, I begged Him to go ahead and deal with everything He could find. I'm sure we're not done yet, but relinquishing my will was a huge spiritual leap for me.

The Old Testament psalmist cried these same prayers. Read Psalm 51:1–12 in the margin. Also read *The Message* translation in the margin on page 123.

According to verse 1, where does God's mercy come from?

_____
_____

What is the source of His capacity to blot out our transgressions?

_____

God's unfailing love and compassion give us mercy when we cry out from our brokenness and ashes.

Read the passage again. Notice the psalmist pleading with God to cleanse away every sin He can find.

Follow the prayer outline in Psalm 51 and ask God to cleanse away every sin in your life. Remember that He is huge in mercy and delights in giving it to you. Write your prayer.

_____

_____

_____

_____

_____

_____

Do you understand that you don't have to beat yourself up any longer? God gives fresh starts generously. He delights in wiping your slate clean. The next time you need His mercy, do not hesitate, do not linger in your own punishment—run into the Father's presence praying Psalm 51! Come with your truth from the inside out and let Him set your broken bones to dancing!

THE CROWN

When a woman stands up at the end of a retreat and talks about the life she used to live and what God is doing for her now, she is saying, "God exchanged my sack of ashes for a crown of beauty. He replaced my despair with an unshakable hope. He keeps wiping away my tears and giving me new reasons to be glad."

Do you know a tender woman who has traded in her worthless ashes for a beautiful crown? List the attributes of that woman.

_____

_____

_____

_____

What makes her so appealing? What draws you to her?

_____

_____

_____

Generous in love—God, give grace! Huge in mercy—wipe out my bad record. Scrub away my guilt, soak out my sins in your laundry. I know how bad I've been; my sins are staring me down. You're the One I've violated, and you've seen it all, seen the full extent of my evil. You have all the facts before you; whatever you decide about me is fair. I've been out of step with you for a long time, in the wrong since before I was born. What you're after is truth from the inside out. Enter me, then; conceive a new, true life. Soak me in your laundry and I'll come out clean, scrub me and I'll have a snow-white life. Tune me in to foot-tapping songs, set these once-broken bones to dancing. Don't look too close for blemishes, give me a clean bill of health. God, make a fresh start in me, shape a Genesis week from the chaos of my life. Don't throw me out with the trash, or fail to breathe holiness in me. Bring me back from gray exile, put a fresh wind in my sails!

Psalm 51:1-12, THE MESSAGE

Look at the list you made and put a star beside the two attributes you'd like God to cultivate in you.

The most powerful thing about the woman underneath the crown is that she never forgets where it came from or how it came to her. The crown was undeserved. It replaced the ashes of brokenness and pain. And in the presence of God, this woman lays her crown at His feet, the feet of the Giver, humbly grateful for His love, mercy, and redemption, thankful for the beauty that has come to cover her days.

God extends the same offer to you and to me. Amazing, but doesn't it sound just like the God we've been talking about? His character is becoming apparent. He always does more. His gifts are lavish and undeserved.

God is truly pursuing you. He is wild for you and longs for your intimacy and affection. He wants you to dance the dance of your life in His arms. He has amazing gifts to give you.

Got some ashes you'd like to trade? The God of heaven is just waiting to see what you'll look like underneath a crown of beauty!

DAY 4

HIS BEAUTIFUL BRIDE

I am 40 years old and for some things, it's probably too late. It's looking as if I will never sing and dance on Broadway. I don't think a letter is coming to invite me to compete in the Olympics. I could still go to law school, but I think I am deciding not to. And the astronaut dream? My heart holds it close but, sadly, too much time has probably passed.

Thankfully, I have always wanted to be more. I want to be courageous and brave. I want to be hospitable and gentle. I want my children to be glad I'm their mother. I desire to be captivating and intelligent. I want to be quick-witted and friendly. I value common sense and lack of pretense. I want to be confident and spiritually secure. I want the clean heart that comes from quick confession. I want my life to matter for the kingdom of heaven. I want to know real grace and give it as freely as my Savior has. I absolutely love that it's never too late to become the woman I have dreamed of being.

Because of Christ, you and I have our whole lives in front of us! Lives meant to be lived for His glory, with desires He placed in our hearts. Longings that call us toward our purpose.

It's never too late to become the woman God has always wanted you to be. He wants you to be His beautiful bride. A woman like you and a woman like me.

Flawed. Insecure. Sometimes downright embarrassing. But not to God. He sees you and me covered by the sacrifice of Christ, and we are beautiful to Him.

How about you? What dreams have probably passed and what dreams still lie in front of you? _____

_____

_____

_____

If you have experienced a day of being the bride, remind yourself what it felt like from the inside out to be lovely and the center of attention. If being the bride hasn't come to you yet, then dream a little. What do you think that day will be like for you?

_____

_____

It's never too late to become the woman God has always wanted you to be.

Here's the wild thing. Because you have chosen Jesus as your Savior, God calls you His bride. Those feelings. The unparalleled beauty and celebration. Being seen and known and desired on a day that comes maybe once in a lifetime. That is the experience of a bride. But He makes us His bride for now and for all eternity.

What amazing imagery God has chosen! A wedding is the height of love, romance, and desire. And God loves us like that forever. Remember the groom and how he anticipates the beauty of his bride? God calls Himself the Bridegroom, and we are His beloved.

The God of heaven desires you as His bride. He anticipates your beauty and delights in your presence. He comes as your lover, your defender, your provider, and your friend. He chose to call you His bride so you could have a picture that accurately reflects the depth and grandeur of His love.

Will you live your life as if you are truly the beautiful bride of Christ?

Does this longing ring true with your soul? ❧ ❑ yes ❑ no ❧
Are you excited about the idea or hesitant? ❧ ❑ excited
❑ hesitant ❧ Why? _____

_____

What obstacles keep you from embracing this truth?

_____

_____

Will you make a commitment right now?

God chose to call you His bride so you could have a picture that accurately reflects the depth and grandeur of His love.

I, _____, with all my heart and soul, commit that by God's help I will live the rest of my life assured that I am His beautiful bride.

Date: _____

Can you imagine how your life will begin to change as you learn to live out of this truth? This is where the wallflower hears the voice of God calling, steps out from the shadows, and begins to dance the dance of her life in the Father's arms.

> *I am 26 years old and already feel I've wasted so much time not grasping or accepting who I am to my Father. I am being swept away by the truth and power of an intensely personal, intimate, loving God.*
> —Tammy

THROUGH THE EYES OF A BRIDE

Let's look at the three characteristics of a bride. Today you are the bride!

You are beautiful. God has called you beautiful, and He loves for you to act on that belief. The women who believe God on this begin acting beautifully and thinking beautifully. They begin to radiate beauty and attract beauty.

How is God prompting you to act more beautifully in your life?

_____

_____

You are confident. Maybe not yet, but as you continue to dance in the arms of God, your confidence will increase. You will begin to act as if you know who is holding you.

Where do you lack confidence? _____

_____

_____

Maybe you need to stop looking over your shoulder. Maybe you need to stop second-guessing yourself. Maybe it's time to hold your head up. However you describe your lack of confidence, pray and ask God for the confidence that comes from a beautiful bride.

_____

_____

You possess unshakable hope. The bride isn't looking back, she is looking forward toward every new day with her groom. When your groom is the King of heaven, you have a lot to look forward to. There is hope. Persevering hope. Anticipating hope. Throw-a-party-and-dance-the-night-away kind of hope!

Proverbs 31:25 says that a woman who knows who she belongs to can "[face] tomorrow with a smile" (THE MESSAGE). Is that how you face tomorrow? Are you hopeful about the days ahead? Do you anticipate the future with gladness?

> How would you describe your hope for the future?
> ❑ no trace of hope, obliterated, zeroed out, all washed up
> ❑ a random flicker of hope, but nothing of substance
> ❑ marginal hope, hopeful that hope is coming
> ❑ restful, get-a-good-night's-sleep, God-has-my-future-and-it-makes-me-smile kind of hope

In her confidence and beauty, the bride hears only the words of promise instead of the whispers of unbelief. She rebukes the bully of Fear and trusts in the devotion she has found. The hope of a bride is steadfast. Stay with these thoughts of the hopeful bride and we'll begin again here tomorrow. Good night, beautiful woman under the crown.

D A Y 5

A BRIDE FULL OF HOPE

I don't think it's coincidence that God uses bridal imagery to refer to the ones He loves. He calls us His bride and says He is our Bridegroom. When we are finally standing in His presence, there will be a celebration in heaven that He calls the "wedding supper of the Lamb" (see Revelation 19:9). God knows the longing of the soul completely. He knows you long to be the bride. How wonderful He is to make it so, for now and for all eternity.

God says when you belong to Him, that means He has made you His beautiful bride. And the bride of Christ possesses an unshakable hope.

The Bible says:

Our hope comes from God (Psalm 62:5).
We can put our hope in His words to us (Psalm 119:74; Romans 15:4).
We can have hope because His love is unfailing (Psalm 147:11).
Our hope comes in the unseen, not what we can see (Romans 8:24).
Jesus, our Savior, is the hope of glory (Colossians 1:27).
Jesus is our blessed hope (Titus 2:13).

"Hallelujah! For our Lord God Almighty reigns. Let us rejoice and be glad and give him glory! For the wedding of the Lamb has come, and his bride has made herself ready. Fine linen, bright and clean, was given her to wear." (Fine linen stands for the righteous acts of the saints.) Then the angel said to me, "Write: 'Blessed are those who are invited to the wedding supper of the Lamb!'"

Revelation 19:6-9

Hope comes from our salvation (1 Thessalonians 5:8).

Hope is an anchor (Hebrews 6:19).

Hope in Jesus purifies us (1 John 3:3).

Look up several of the previous passages in your Bible. Do you place your hope in your retirement account, in your chosen career, or in your possessions? Where do you find your hope? _____

_____

_____

_____

_____

If the Scriptures are true and our hope is refilled by the presence of God in our lives, His unfailing love, and our salvation, then what are you having difficulty believing? _____

_____

_____

I want to be able to smile at tomorrow, but apart from hope I will cower in fear. The bride of Christ is full of hope because she knows the Bridegroom is wild about her. Because of His love, they can face anything the future holds. The smile on her face as she walks toward Him comes from the hope she has placed in His love.

As God has been speaking to you about His love for you, how is your hope being changed? I am praying for your soul to be renewed by the kind of love that a beautiful bride has for her Groom.

THE PRINCESS COMPLEX

I don't know where you are on this princess complex thing. Some women are really into the whole princess idea. I have to admit it is incredibly appealing to me, but I have always denied myself the desire to be cared for in such a special and lavish way.

Read the words of Scripture that tell us how the King, the God who pursues us and tells us we are beautiful, wants to treat the woman He adores:

> Wedding gifts pour in from Tyre;
>   rich guests shower you with presents.
> (Her wedding dress is dazzling, lined with gold by the
>   weavers;
> All her dresses and robes are woven with gold.
> She is led to the king,
>   followed by her virgin companions.

A procession of joy and laughter!

  a grand entrance to the king's palace!)

    Psalm 45:12-15, The Message

Obviously the King wants to treat the beautiful princess bride with extravagance. Can you believe that's how God wants to treat you? Not just some woman back in Tyre, but you. He truly wants to shower you with the gifts of His riches.

> Can you embrace this truth about how the King wants to treat you or do you still push it away? ❏ I can embrace it. ❏ I still have a hard time believing it applies to me.

You really have only two options: to believe or to continue in the frailty of doubt. What if you get to heaven and find out everything God said to you in the Bible was really true? Won't you wish you had lived in that truth? Why regret any longer the years wasted in disbelief? Don't miss the freedom and strength that come from believing so deeply that you have left no other options.

How is God showing you that each of the following is true in your life?

You are beautiful. _____

_____

_____

You are desired. _____

_____

_____

You are held. _____

_____

_____

You are protected. _____

_____

_____

You are rescued. _____

_____

_____

You are forgiven. _____

_____

You are pursued. _____
_____
_____

You are seen. _____
_____
_____

You are precious. _____
_____
_____

You are His princess. _____
_____
_____

You are His beautiful bride. _____
_____
_____

THE DANCE

So what will you do?

Will you continue to

stand around the edge of

your life? Or will you

get yourself on the dance

floor and dance the dance

of your life in His arms?

Well, my friend, our time together is winding down, and it's time for you to make a decision. You have heard that God calls you beautiful. You hear His voice calling you into His arms. I think you can just about hear the music, and you are finally willing to admit that those feet of yours can't wait to dance. So what will you do? Will you continue to stand around the edge of your life? Or will you get yourself on the dance floor and dance the dance of your life in His arms?

Spend some time in prayer about this. Journal. Call someone. But don't miss responding to God. He is inviting you to dance. What will you say? If you listen with your heart, what do you hear God saying to you? _____
_____
_____
_____
_____
_____
_____
_____

THE WOMAN IN HIS ARMS

If you are the beautiful bride of Christ, and you are, then it's time to shine. It's time for you and me to begin acting like we belong to God. It's time to let ourselves fully become the woman in His arms.

Enough of the weak-willed woman. Enough of the distant country. Enough standing around acting as though we are just one of the girls from the kingdom. Enough of the ashes. Enough fear, lies, shame, and guilt. Enough of the church lady.

I want to be desperate for Jesus. I want to run to Him as He runs to me. I want to want Him more than I want anything else. I want to be changed from this shabby woman into a likeness that bears His resemblance. I want to declare for now and for all my days that my heart is fully His.

Write your own declaration. Make copies and put this declaration of love and freedom in places where you'll reread it often. _____

My friend, my fellow journey woman, my co-dancer, may I pray for you?

> *Oh, Sweet Jesus,*
> *Please take the heart of this tender woman and care for it deeply. Hold her closer than she has ever known. Speak to her in ways that astound her. Remind her of Your presence in light and in darkness. Comfort her with Your tender mercy. God, please let her dance the dance of her life in Your arms! Let her know the freedom You have given her from Your grace. Change her from encounter to encounter into Your likeness. Help her believe You call her beautiful. Give her a confidence she has never known apart from You. And God, let her glimpse with her new eyes the hope You have set before her.*
> *In Your name and for Your renown, amen.*

Run with all you have into His arms. I can't wait to meet you and hear about the dance.

---

1. Nicole Johnson, *Stepping into the Ring* (Nashville: Thomas Nelson, 2003).

Leader Guide

This leader guide will help you facilitate the small-group sessions for *Do You Think I'm Beautiful?* A leader kit is also available (item 005035527) containing two DVDs with Angela's accompanying video messages to be used during the small-group sessions. While the video sessions will greatly enrich your study, you may choose to use only the member book.

If you are leading this study without the accompanying video messages, the introductory session is optional. Having an introductory session offers a time to distribute the member book and get acquainted. If you choose not to have an introductory session, make certain participants receive their workbooks in time to complete week 1 before group session 1.

If you are using the accompanying video messages in your study, offer an introductory session for all women who think they might be interested in participating in this study. No member book is needed for this session.

The leader guide also contains plans for an optional celebration session. This is a time when the women can come together, share food and fellowship, and discuss the things that have meant the most to them in their study of *Do You Think I'm Beautiful?* For those groups using the videos, this session provides a time to show the celebration feature on the DVD.

Do You Think I'm Beautiful? is an excellent study for women who have not yet made the decision to follow Christ as Savior as well as new Christians and women who have been Christians for many years. Take full advantage of this opportunity to invite women from your community

and to encourage women in your church to bring their friends and relatives. This study deals with thoughts and feelings shared by women young and old; single, married, divorced, or widowed; secular or Christian. Women may be introduced to Jesus for the first time or think about their relationship with Him in new ways.

Consider options for meeting times and places. You may have one large group view the videos at church and then move to small groups for discussion, or you may choose to meet in women's homes throughout the week. Both options will work well.

Beginning with an introductory session can accomplish several things:

- You can get an idea of how many women will attend and get additional books as needed.
- You can offer study groups at a variety of dates, times, and settings to fit women's busy schedules.
- You can determine when child care will be needed.
- You can encourage women to invite friends and relatives, both Christian and non-Christian, to the study.
- You can find out how many small-group leaders will be needed.
- Women who are undecided about the study because they don't know other women well will have the opportunity to meet women, begin relationships, and see that they will have positive experiences in this study.

Ask God to put together the small groups He desires for this study. Announce the study in the church newsletter, worship bulletin, on hallway bulletin boards, and during women's ministry activities. Use the promotional segment on DVD disk 1 to encourage participation.

Provide child care for each session if needed. Before each session, arrange to have a DVD player in your meeting room.

Complete each week's assignments, and encourage all women to take the time daily to read the material for that day, to reflect on questions asked, and to write their answers. They will receive much more benefit from the study by participating fully through the six weeks of study.

As the leader you do not have to have all the answers, but you need to be familiar with the material. This leader guide is designed to be used for 60–90-minute small-group sessions. You can set the format and time frame of your group session based on how much time you wish to allow for discussion. Don't feel you have to cover every activity in this leader guide. Many more discussion starters are offered each week than you will be able to cover in a single session. Be flexible. Consider the personality of your group as you make decisions about which topics to discuss. Allow the Lord to lead your group discussions.

If the number of women wanting to meet for study at one time and place is too large for meaningful discussion, consider breaking into smaller groups of four to six for discussion. Small groups meeting at the same time and place can come together as a larger group to view the video.

INTRODUCTORY SESSION

Before the Study

1. Read "About the Author" (p. 4) and the introduction (p. 5). Be prepared to introduce the author, the study, and the format.

2. Have copies of *Do You Think I'm Beautiful?* ready for distribution.

3. You may choose to decorate your meeting room similar to the one shown each week during the introductory segment of the video—with balloons and streamers.

4. Make plans to have refreshments if you choose. If you follow the decorations theme, simple punch and cookies would work well.

During the Session

1. Welcome women as they arrive.

2. Introduce yourself and, depending on the familiarity of the group, give a little information about yourself. Create a casual, nonthreatening atmosphere for the women. Explain that this is an opportunity for them to get an introduction to Angela and her message. After this session they may choose whether they wish to continue in the next six weeks of study. Depending on the size of your group, they may also choose the date, time, and place they wish to participate in the study.

3. Introduce Angela Thomas and the message of the study.

4. Show the introductory video session.

5. Read Romans 8:38-39. Reiterate that Angela's focus in this study is on strength and joy.

6. Have a time of reflection. Pose these questions, but don't ask for a response: *Do you long to know that someone truly sees you as beautiful? Do you want to move in the dance of life from wallflower to active participant? If you've felt these longings—the need for a meaningful, intimate, relationship with someone who sees you as beautiful, the need to move from the sidelines of life to fulfilling your passions—this study is for you! You are invited to dance with the Father. He longs to tell you how beautiful He thinks you are! During this study women will find healing from past hurts, develop spiritual community with other women, and open the doors to a closer relationship with Jesus.*

7. Consider having prayer partners during the weeks of this study. Women will have differ-

ent comfort levels in sharing from their hearts. Some will share openly in small groups, but others may not. Some may share more comfortably one-on-one. All women can partner to pray for each other that they will see themselves more clearly and draw closer to God as a result of this study.

8. Have a time of prayer. Ask God to help women live like they belong to Him and know that He loves them. Thank Him for seeing each woman as beautiful, just as He created her to be. Ask Him to help each woman begin to see her own beauty, knowing that she is loved by God. Lead women to spend some time praying silently, asking God to lead them during this study to (1) grow in their understanding of themselves and their relationship with God through Jesus Christ, and (2) to grow in relationship to other women in the group.

9. Explain the format of the study. The member books provide a daily reading and reflection for five days a week for the six weeks of the study. Each week of homework is followed by a small-group meeting to see a video segment with additional, related content from Angela and discussion about what they have done during the week.

10. Give each participant approximately 10 Post-It® notes. Select pastel colors and a size big enough to write the verses. Allow time for them to write Colossians 1:10-12 on one sheet. Suggest that women place these verses on their bathroom mirrors throughout the study. Verses will be highlighted each week. As they study during the week as well as in group study, they can write verses and add them around the edge of the mirror. If other family members use the same bathroom, they can also benefit from the chosen Scriptures. Provide more Post-It® notes as needed.

11. Give the women an opportunity to purchase or receive member books. Let them know that books will be available throughout the week and during the first session if they need more time to make a decision. If members are responsible for paying for their books, offer to collect the money or enlist someone in advance to do this.

12. Assign week 1 for the next small-group session. Encourage participants to complete each learning activity to get the most out of this study.

SESSION 1

Before the Session

1. Prepare an attendance sheet for participants to sign their names, addresses, phone numbers, and e-mail addresses. Place this sheet on a table with pens, markers, and name tags. You'll need a felt-tip pen for each woman.

2. Have member books available for newcomers.

3. Complete the week 1 material and preview the video for session 1.

4. Get oval-shaped balloons. Print out the following verses on white paper: Job 36:7; Psalm 34:4-5; Psalm 45:10-11; Psalm 51:6; Psalm 68:5; Psalm 139:1-3; Psalm 139:13-16; Psalm 145:18; Jeremiah 29:11; Zephaniah 3:17; Matthew 7:7-12; John 8:28; John 10:29; John 10:32; John 14:16-17; Ephesians 1:2; Ephesians 2:4-8; James 1:17; 1 John 1:9; 1 John 4:17-18. Cut apart the Scripture portions. Carefully roll the paper strip and insert each one in a balloon. Blow up the balloons and tie them. You should have at least 20 balloons for the 20 Scripture portions. In addition, you will need a few more balloons than the total number of women. These Scriptures were all used in this week's study. If your time is limited, select the Scripture passages you want to discuss and type and place in the balloons only the Scriptures you want to read and discuss during this small-group session.

5. If your church has the necessary licensure, plan to show one or more video clips from the movie *Cinderella,* perhaps a scene with Cinderella and her stepmother and stepsisters, a scene of the prince and Cinderella at the ball, and the scene where Cinderella slips her foot into the glass slipper near the end of the movie. Prepare in advance so that you can find the scenes quickly during the session. For this and other suggested times using movie clips, if you do not have permission, simply tell about the movie.

6. As women arrive, play music that is upbeat and joyful.

During the Session

1. Before women arrive, begin to play the music. Scatter balloons around the floor of the meeting room.

2. As participants arrive, ask them to sign in, prepare name tags, and pick up copies of the member book if they don't already have one. Offer to collect the money.

3. Encourage women to chat informally as women continue to arrive. Invite them to talk about a time when they felt beautiful.

4. When all have arrived and have had a few minutes to share their memories of being beautiful, ask women if they were ever told, "Pretty is as pretty does." Ask: *What did that message mean to you?*

5. Invite them to recall the story of *Cinderella.* Show video clips if available. Invite women to discuss using questions like these: *When have you felt that you did not belong, that you were on the edge of the room or the wallflower at the dance? When have you felt surprised and thrilled to be chosen, found beautiful, included in the dance of life? When have you acted like an ugly stepmother or stepsister? When have you affirmed or helped someone else like a wonderful fairy godmother? Which role is most familiar to you? Which role do you most long for?*

6. Point out that women may be more likely to remember their wallflower moments in life and to see them as the truth about themselves; they are amazed at the times someone has seen them as beautiful and do not see that as the norm for their lives.

7. Distribute felt-tip pens. Invite women to pick up a balloon and to write one negative word on the balloon that represents a memory of feeling less than beautiful. Then, as you play music, invite them to toss the balloons to one another. After a minute or less, invite them to grab another balloon and to write another negative word that they may have used to describe themselves. Continue this pattern of writing and tossing the balloons until three or four words have been written on balloons. If a balloon bursts, just continue. That's the reason for beginning with a few extra balloons. Then while you continue to play the music, invite women to stomp and break the balloons, obliterating the negative words and messages they have carried that keep them from seeing themselves as loved and beautiful. Then ask them to pick up the Scripture passages.

8. Invite women to read the Scriptures one at a time. Ask all the women to share what each Scripture meant to them during their daily study time.

9. Ask women to turn to the viewer guide on page 7 of their member books and take notes as they watch the video. Show video session 1.

10. Read again Psalm 139:1-3. Ask women to write these verses on a Post-It® note to place on their bathroom mirrors along with any other of this session's verses that were especially meaningful.

11. Close in prayer, thanking God for the moments when we felt beautiful in His sight and when we truly knew and acknowledged His love for us.

12. Assign week 2 for the next small-group session.

SESSION 2

Before the Session

1. Complete the week 2 material and preview the session 2 video.
2. Provide paper and pens for each participant.
3. Create a display with several containers of unlikely or inappropriate and contrasting contents. For example, a beautiful vase filled with dirt, an old jar with a beautiful flower, a coffee mug filled with rocks, and so forth.
4. Have a chalkboard, whiteboard, or flipchart available.
5. Provide extra Bibles as needed.

During the Session

1. Welcome the women as they arrive. Invite them to form small groups of three or four and to talk about objects that are beautiful to them. When everyone has arrived and had opportunity to participate, ask groups to share some of the objects they find beautiful. Invite them to comment briefly on why they consider these objects beautiful.
2. Now ask them to name physical attributes they consider beautiful. Observe as women comment whether they tend to name characteristics of people unlike themselves. For example, a petite woman may say that she sees women who are tall as beautiful. If women are generally naming attributes that better describe others than themselves, when you draw this part of the discussion to a close, comment on your observation. Then tell this story: *Two women worked together and became friends. One of the women had thin legs; the other had heavier legs and always admired and envied her friend's thin legs. One day around the time of year to shop for swimsuits, the woman with the thin legs talked about how much she hated her thin, "shapeless"* legs. *A serious childhood illness had affected her ability to walk and had impacted the lack of muscle development in her legs. She had always hated the very attribute the other woman envied.* Conclude by saying: *Women often find it easier to see beauty in others than in themselves.*

3. Now ask women to think of a woman who is beautiful. They may choose whether to name the person or not, but ask them to describe why they see this woman as beautiful. Listen and observe whether the attributes they list are physical or have more to do with who the woman is, her character and Christlikeness. You may want to list on a piece of paper the attributes they are including as they speak. Do not write these on the chalkboard or whiteboard at this time. When women have finished sharing about the beautiful women in their lives, write on the board the kinds of attributes they have listed. Note that the women may or may not have been beauty contest winners, but all were beautiful because of who they were in relationship to God and to others. Transition by saying that healthy relationships with others make life richer.

4. Draw women's attention to the display you have created. Ask them what is wrong with it. The answer is that containers are filled with unlikely or inappropriate objects. The containers were designed for other purposes. Then say: *God created us with a longing for Him. Only a relationship with God through Jesus Christ will fill our deepest longings. Yet we constantly try to fill the emptiness or hunger in our lives with something besides God.* Invite women to name things women use to satisfy their longings. List these on the board or flipchart. They may include things like shopping, drugs, food, and so on. Affirm their answers. Add, if they don't, that expecting another person—whether a friend, spouse, or parent—to fill our emptiness or meet our every needs turns human relationships from healthy to unhealthy. Even our closest friend

or a wonderful mate cannot satisfy our deepest needs, the need to have an intimate relationship with God, the very purpose for which we were created. Expecting to have our needs met by an object, an experience, or another person will all lead to frustration. Human relationships are important, but ultimately our relationships with God last throughout eternity while others may fail or end.

5. Some women in your group may not be Christians (or you may not know whether they are). Mention that if women want to discuss their personal relationship with God, you will be available after the session to talk with them, to schedule a time to talk with them, or to arrange an appointment at their convenience with a minister.

6. Invite women to turn in their member books to page 41, the list of characteristics of God. Then ask them to turn in their Bibles to Psalm 8:9 and read this verse in various translations. Invite them to paraphrase the verse to express their need for God in their lives. For example, "O Lord, my Lord, how comforting is Your name in my heart." Or, "O Lord, my God, how satisfying is Your name in my life." Or, "O Lord, our Lord, how calling and motivating and challenging is Your name in my church." Or, "O Lord, our Lord, how needed is Your name in my community." Suggest that women pray this prayer throughout the coming week when they think about how God fulfills their greatest longings and supplies their needs through His power, protection, peace, and provision.

7. Read Luke 8:47. Ask women to write the verse on a Post-It® note to place on their bathroom mirrors. Suggest that they also write any other verses from this week's study that have been meaningful to them.

8. Ask participants to turn to the viewer guide on page 29 and take notes as they watch the video. Show video session 2.

9. Close in prayer. Thank God for creating in the heart of every woman, man, boy, and girl a longing for Him that can be filled in no other way. Pray that women gathered here will turn nowhere else to satisfy the needs that only He can fulfill.

10. Assign week 3 for the next small-group session.

SESSION 3

Before the Session

1. Complete the week 3 material and preview the session 3 video. Read through the plans for this week's session.

2. Provide paper, pens, and large felt-tip markers for each participant.

3. Check your supply of Post-It® notes, and make sure you have more available as needed.

4. Have a chalkboard, whiteboard, or flipchart available.

5. Provide extra Bibles as needed.

6. Plan to have music playing as women arrive. Make it as loud as is tolerable for a short time.

7. Gather a lot of large cardboard boxes. Scatter these around the room so that the room looks cluttered and it is difficult for women to walk.

During the Session

1. Have the music blaring as women arrive. Act as if you are unaware of the loud music.

2. Welcome women as they arrive. Speak softly so that it is difficult for them to hear you. Suggest that they enter and visit one another.

3. When you are ready to begin, quietly call women together. Then suddenly turn off the music and again tell the women that you are ready to begin.

4. Read 1 Kings 19:11-12. Ask the women if they could hear God's voice when they came into the

room. Let them talk about the noise. Respond that they will be talking about noise as one problem that keeps us from hearing God.

5. Ask them if anything else is distracting them from focusing on God. When they comment on the boxes, say that clutter in our lives also often keeps us from hearing from God. Invite them to look through week 3 to identify things in our lives that might cause clutter or noise. Ask them to take their felt-tip markers and write these clutter- and noise-makers on the boxes, using large letters. As they do, ask them to stack the boxes against a wall so that everyone can see the words written. Make sure all the items on the lists on page 62 are included as well as other ideas from this week and ideas the women add to the list. Write more than one item per box as needed. If duplicate words are written by different women, the duplication will reinforce the idea of clutter. When women pause from their writing, ask them to look at the wall and see if they can add any additional clutter that may be in their lives or the lives of other women. Then comment that like the wall of boxes, clutter in our lives becomes a barrier to communication with God. Both clutter and noise keep us from hearing what God has to say to us.

6. Note that there is one other barrier to hearing from God, and that barrier is interference from Satan. He is the source of lies. Ask the women to brainstorm miscommunications, distortions of the truth, and outright lies that come from the devil. Write these on the boxes or on a whiteboard, flipchart, or chalkboard.

7. Read the first part of 2 Timothy 1:7. Invite other women to read this verse from their Bibles, using several translations until both "timidity" and "fear" are named as not coming from God. Ask the women to think about how fear and timidity are from the Devil. Ask how fear and timidity can keep women from serving God or even believing God. Then continue

reading from 2 Timothy 1:7 (also from several translations) the gifts listed that are from God. Write these on the board or flipchart. Then ask the women to add other good gifts that come from God. List these also. Ask how these gifts enable us to serve God better.

8. Ask the women to get in groups of three or with their prayer partner and talk about times when they have heard the voice of God. Tell them to include times when they may have sensed God's Spirit communicating with them during a worship service, when they were reading the Bible, when they were praying, when they were listening to music, when they experienced Him in His creation, or through the ministry of another person. Ask them to think of times when they have sensed God's peace, His presence, His provision, or His protection. After the women have had an opportunity to talk among themselves, ask them to volunteer to tell about times God has spoken to them. Make sure they understand that God speaks in many different ways to different people. Read Jeremiah 29:13. Point out that people who hear God are the ones who seek Him and are listening to hear Him speak.

9. Ask women to work in small groups of four or six (combining prayer partners or two small groups) to make two lists: (1) things they can do to unclutter their lives and reduce the noise in their lives; and (2) things they can do to seek God and hear His voice. After a few minutes invite women to share ideas from their lists.

10. Read 2 Corinthians 12:9. Comment that God will help us when we are struggling to overcome Satan's lies and to believe the truth from God's Word. Ask women to write the verse on a Post-It® note to place on their bathroom mirrors. Suggest that they also write any other verses from this week's study that have been particularly meaningful.

11. Ask participants to turn to the viewer guide on page 51 and take notes as they watch the video. Show video session 3.

12. Close in prayer, thanking God for choosing to communicate with those of us who seek Him. Pray that women will be able to reduce the noise and clutter in their lives and to listen for God's voice.

13. Assign week 4 for the next small-group session.

SESSION 4

Before the Session

1. Complete the week 4 material and preview the session 4 video. Read through the plans for this week's session.

2. Provide paper, pens, and large felt-tip markers for each participant.

3. Check your supply of Post-It® notes to make sure you have them available as needed.

4. Have a chalkboard, whiteboard, or flipchart available.

5. Provide extra Bibles as needed.

6. Display a variety of empty vases—regular vases as well as those that would hold a large bouquet, rose bowls, and so forth. Out of sight have an arrangement of some beautiful flowers and some weeds or some flowers that are dying and detract from the beauty of the bouquet. Leftover flowers from last Sunday or the week before may serve this purpose.

7. If possible, provide stems of a variety of flowers and greenery, enough for every woman to have one stem.

8. At the end of the session, women will put flowers in vases. Be prepared with vases that can be given away. Have names and addresses of members who are sick and/or homebound members. Plan to enlist women to deliver the vases of flowers.

9. In advance, enlist a woman to role play, read dramatically, or tell the story of the woman caught in adultery in John 8:2-12.

During the Session

1. Welcome women as they arrive. Draw their attention to the empty vases. Give them paper and pencil or pen and ask them to draw a single flower or one of the vases with flowers in it. Women will protest that they are not artists, but assure them that this is not a competition for artistic skills.

2. When all have arrived and had opportunity to draw, ask women to tell what kinds of flowers they drew and which vases they used. Point out that beauty comes in different shapes, sizes, colors, and fragrances. And when they come together, they create a beautiful aroma, just like this group of women.

3. Point out that these vases are empty. Ask women to think about these vases as their lives. Ask: *If your lives were empty of characteristics, past experiences that shape who you are today, or messages or tapes that you hear from the past, what kinds of characteristics would you like to fill your lives?* As they name the characteristics, write them on the board.

4. Now display the mixed bouquet of beautiful flowers and weeds or dying flowers. Point out that most of our lives are like the bouquet, a mixture of beauty and items we would like to weed out of our lives. Ask the group to name the kinds of things women would like to weed out of their lives. Word the question so that it is not personal, so that women can brainstorm freely without owning the traits she names. Items should include words like *depression, fear, guilt, anger, doubt, defeat, sin, arrogance,* and *being judgmental.* They may also mention words from other weeks like *busyness.*

5. Ask a volunteer to read Galatians 5:1. Point out that when our lives are filled with these weeds, we are weighed down. But ridding ourselves of the negatives in our lives will only leave us as empty vessels unless we choose to add Christlike characteristics. Ask another to read Psalm 103:12. Assure women that God is always ready to forgive and forget our sin. He removes our sin as far from us as east is from west and remembers it no more. When we continually focus on past sins in our lives, we doubt God and block ourselves from receiving all the love He has to give us.

6. Introduce the woman who will present the story of the woman caught in adultery (John 8:2-12). Follow the story with a discussion with questions like these: *Did Jesus judge the woman? What did He tell her to do? What was Jesus saying about judging others?* Compare this story with the story of the prodigal son. End the discussion with verse 12. Ask: *How do sin and other negatives in our lives bring darkness that blocks out the light?*

7. Ask a volunteer to read 1 John 4:16-18. Invite women to focus on verse 18 and to think about the negative characteristic in their own lives that they would like to eliminate. Ask them to discuss how fear or other negatives in their lives are a kind of punishment. Ask: *If punishment is viewed as being like time-out or withholding privileges, what do the negatives in life keep us from doing?* Record their answers. They should include: trusting God fully; serving God fully; maximizing our gifts; loving others fully; loving God with all our hearts, souls, mind, and strength.

8. Ask them to write 1 John 4:18 on a Post-It® note to place on their mirrors. Then ask them to write it substituting the word *fear* with the negative they'd like to remove from their lives.

9. Ask a volunteer to read 2 Timothy 2:22. Ask the women to write this verse on a Post-It® note and place it on their bathroom mirrors.

10. Ask participants to turn to the viewer guide on page 71 and take notes as they watch the video. Show video session 4.

11. Spread the flowers on a table. Invite women to choose one that she thinks is beautiful, perhaps one like she drew at the beginning of the session. As a sign of her commitment to seek God's help to weed the negatives from her life, ask her to add the flower to those of some of the other women and to create a beautiful bouquet, like women created in God's image. Ask for volunteers to take flowers to women in the hospital or those who are homebound.

12. Close in prayer. Thank God for creating beautiful women. Pray that He will help them to have confidence in their beauty by receiving His love and casting out fear and other weeds in their lives.

13. Assign week 5 for the next small-group session.

SESSION 5

Before the Session

1. Complete the week 5 material and preview the session 5 video. Read through the plans for this week's session.

2. Provide paper, pens, and large felt-tip markers for each participant.

3. Make sure your supply of Post-It® notes is adequate for the session.

4. Have a chalkboard, whiteboard, or flipchart available.

5. Provide extra Bibles as needed.

6. If your church has a license to show video clips, secure a copy of *You've Got Mail*. Find and mark these segments so you can get to them quickly. You will not use them in the order in which they appear in the movie: (1) the scene where Kathleen Kelly (Meg Ryan) is sick and

she and Joe Fox (Tom Hanks) talk about, "It's not personal; it's business." She goes on to say, "All that means is it's not personal to you, but it's personal to me"; (2) the scene where Kathleen sends the e-mail about her store closing and how she feels like her mother is dying all over again; and the scene where the mother and daughter are twirling in the store, a memory of Kathleen just before she turns off the lights and locks her store for the last time; (3) the scene where the book store employees are at lunch at Birdie Conrad's (Jean Stapleton), where she asks Kathleen Kelly what she plans to do. Kathleen replies, in defeat, that she plans to close the store; Birdie responds, "You're daring to dream a new life"; the scene where Kathleen and Joe Fox meet and talk about the children's book she is writing; she says, "If I didn't have all this free time, I would never have discovered …"; (4) the scene where Joe goes to visit Kathleen when she has a cold; she asks why he is there, and he answers, "I want to be your friend."

7. Prepare Ephesians 3:14-21 so women can read it together. Type and distribute it or use PowerPoint.

During the Session

1. Welcome women as they arrive. Ask them to form small groups and answer these questions: *What is the scariest, most risk-taking thing you've ever done (or done lately)? How did you find the courage to do it? What happened because you took this risk? What might have happened if you had not taken this risk? What good things resulted?* Write the questions on the board or a flipchart where women can see them. Or, direct their attention to the last paragraph on page 107, and ask them, in small groups, to write a country music song to the tune of their choice about weak-willed women.

2. After all have arrived and had opportunity to participate, lead a discussion about risk-taking

or ask small groups to sing their country song. Affirm their efforts.

3. Using the clips from *You've Got Mail*, lead a discussion with these corresponding parts: (1) Ask a volunteer to read Matthew 5:45. Discuss the fact that everyone faces crises and tragedies in their lives. Some may be completely unavoidable; some we may bring on ourselves. Regardless, God is with us in every situation. Ask a volunteer to read Exodus 19:4. (2) At this point Kathleen Kelly is closing the door to something she has known all her life, her book store. At the time she does not feel like dancing, but she holds on to the memory of dancing with her mother. Ask volunteers to read Psalm 73:23 and Isaiah 41:13. Point out that having a strong foundation of faith helps people get through crises. (3) Point out that often what appears to be an ending is a new beginning that is greater than anything we could have imagined. Ask volunteers to read Psalm 25:5; Psalm 33:22; Psalm 42:5; Psalm 62:5; Psalm 71:5; Psalm 130:5; Isaiah 40:31; Jeremiah 29:11; Romans 4:18; Romans 12:12; 2 Corinthians 3:12; Hebrews 6:19a; Hebrews 10:23; Hebrews 11:1. (4) Who in your life needs a friend right now? Ask a volunteer to read Ephesians 4:32; Ephesians 5:19; 1 Thessalonians 5:11; 1 John 4:7.

4. Ask the women to share verses that represent God's promises, verses that have meaning in their own difficult times. Be prepared to read or ask volunteers to read verses to get started or to fill a lull in sharing: Exodus 19:4; Psalm 23:1-4; Psalm 27:1; Psalm 46:1-2; Matthew 23:37; Matthew 28:20b; Romans 8:38-39; or other verses from this week's study.

5. Some women may be going through a difficult time right now. Others may openly carry the baggage from past painful experiences while others secretly hide the scars of their hurts. Invite women to take paper and pen and write a letter to God. They may want to thank Him

for a painful ending in life that became a beautiful new beginning. They may want to ask His help in putting fear behind them and renewing their hope. Tell them that they will not be asked to share these personal letters.

6. Ask those who are interested in a women's retreat as suggested in this week's study to raise their hands. If a number of women are interested, ask for a few volunteers to plan a retreat following this study.

7. Ask a volunteer to read Romans 5:5. Affirm that God never disappoints. Ask the women to write this verse on a Post-It® note and place it on their bathroom mirrors.

8. Ask participants to turn to the viewer guide on page 93 and take notes as they watch the video. Show video session 5.

9. Close in prayer, reading aloud Ephesians 3:14-21. You may also choose to ask women to read it together. If you do this, project the words using PowerPoint or have them written where all can read the same translation together.

10. Assign week 6 for the next session.

SESSION 6

Before the Session

1. Complete the week 6 material and preview the session 6 video. Read through the plans for this week's session.

2. Provide paper, pens, and large felt-tip markers for each participant.

3. Check your supply of Post-It® notes to make sure you have enough available.

4. Have a chalkboard, whiteboard, or flipchart available.

5. Provide extra Bibles as needed.

6. If your church is licensed to do so, plan to show clips from the movie *My Big Fat Greek Wedding*. Be prepared to show the scene early

in the movie where Toula Portokalos (Nia Vardalos) is working in the family restaurant and Ian Miller (John Corbett) comes in; also find the scene where Ian suggests they go to a Greek restaurant and she refers to herself as "frump girl," and he responds that he never saw her as frump girl but as someone different and interesting.

7. Enlist a woman to role-play or to tell the story of Esther. Include references to both her inner and outer beauty. Point out that she took a great risk to save her people.

During the Session

1. Welcome women as they arrive. Ask them to recall the beginning of this study when they shared a time when they felt beautiful. Ask them to form small groups and share a time when they did not feel beautiful, then share again a time when they did feel beautiful. Point out that every woman has both kinds of times. Note that she often feels beautiful when she feels loved. Ask a volunteer to read Psalm 45:11.

2. Show the clips from *My Big Fat Greek Wedding*. Note the changes in Toula's appearance. Part of the change was because she felt loved, but part of it was also because she was growing through education and career. She had added purpose and meaning in her life.

3. Ask a volunteer to read Isaiah 52:7. Even women who truly see themselves as beautiful have a difficult time seeing their feet as beautiful. Yet feet with the purpose of taking the good news to those who need to hear are truly beautiful because they are on mission to serve the King. Then read and lead a discussion on Isaiah 61:1-3, using content from this week's study.

4. Introduce the woman who will tell about Esther, a beautiful queen. After the presentation, ask questions for discussion: *How did Esther's physical beauty open doors for her to help her people? What risks did she take? Was she afraid? How did*

she overcome her fear? In what ways was Esther beautiful on the inside?

5. Ask a volunteer to read Isaiah 62:5b. Ask the women to write this verse on a Post-It® note and place it on their bathroom mirrors.

6. Ask participants to turn to the viewer guide on page 113 and take notes as they watch the video. Show video session 6.

7. Announce plans for next week's celebration to conclude the study of *Do You Think I'm Beautiful?* Enlist women to bring refreshments.

8. Close in prayer using the prayer on page 131. Adapt the prayer to fit your context.

CELEBRATION SESSION

Before the Session

1. Plan to give women a day to focus on being beautiful inside and out. Have stations set up for manicures, pedicures, shoulder massages, makeovers, color assessments, nutrition tips, fitness ideas for busy women, making posters with special Bible verses from this study (you can use these in church classrooms), ideas for enriching your prayer life, journaling, and tips on sharing the gospel. Stations should plan to rotate every 15 minutes. Some businesses may be willing to supply products and/or personnel to advertise their business. Teenage girls may help with manicures or plan a fashion show for women (make sure it's age appropriate for the women in your group).

2. Check to make sure members are bringing refreshments. Provide paper products, ice, and other non-food items.

3. Preview the bonus video.

4. Prepare to share information about any upcoming events for women in your church.

During the Session

1. Welcome women to the celebration of beauty. Point out the various stations where women can choose to be pampered and become more beautiful on the inside and the outside.

2. Show the bonus video.

3. Ask women to share what they have gained from this study. Ask them to share Bible verses that have become more significant to them during this study.

4. Ask the women if they would like to plan another group Bible study. For options, visit *www.lifeway.com*.

5. If the women have planned a retreat, share information about date, time, and place.

6. Thank participants for coming and for sharing from their lives.

7. Close in prayer, thanking God for these beautiful women.

CHRISTIAN GROWTH STUDY PLAN

In the **Christian Growth Study Plan**, *Do You Think I'm Beautiful?* is a resource for course credit in the subject area Home and Family of the Christian Growth category of plans. To receive credit, read the book, complete the learning activities, show your work to your pastor, a staff member or church leader, then complete the following information. This page may be duplicated. Send the completed page to:

Christian Growth Study Plan
One LifeWay Plaza; Nashville, TN 37234-0117
FAX: (615)251-5067; E-mail: *cgspnet@lifeway.com*

For information about the Christian Growth Study Pl[ ] refer to the Christian Growth Study Plan Catalog onli[ ] at *www.lifeway.com/cgsp*. If you do not have access[ ] the Internet, contact the Christian Growth Study Pl[ ] office at (800) 968-5519 for the specific plan you ne[ ] for your ministry.

DO YOU THINK I'M BEAUTIFUL?
CG-1312

PARTICIPANT INFORMATION

Social Security Number (USA ONLY-optional)	Personal CGSP Number*	Date of Birth (MONTH, DAY, YEAR)

Name (First, Middle, Last)	Home Phone	

Address (Street, Route, or P.O. Box)	City, State, or Province	Zip/Postal Code

Email Address for CGSP use

Please check appropriate box: ❏ Resource purchased by church ❏ Resource purchased by self ❏ Other

CHURCH INFORMATION

Church Name

Address (Street, Route, or P.O. Box)	City, State, or Province	Zip/Postal Code

CHANGE REQUEST ONLY

☐ Former Name		
☐ Former Address	City, State, or Province	Zip/Postal Code
☐ Former Church	City, State, or Province	Zip/Postal Code

Signature of Pastor, Conference Leader, or Other Church Leader	Date

*New participants are requested but not required to give SS# and date of birth. Existing participants, please give CGSP# when using SS# for the first time. Thereafter, only one ID# is required. **Mail to:** Christian Growth Study Plan, One LifeWay Plaza, Nashville, TN 37234-0117. Fax: (615)251-5067.

Revised[ ]